A FIRST LOOK AT THE

USA

A CULTURAL READER

MILADA BROUKAL

LONGMAN

A First Look at the USA: A Cultural Reader

Addison Wesley Longman, 10 Bank Street, White Plains, NY 10606

Photo credits: Pages 13 and 54, Wright Bros. airplane, © National Air &
    Space Museum, Smithsonian Institution, Photo No. A 26767 B-2; pages 25
    and 27, McDonald's restaurant, McDonald's Corporation; pages 60 and 66,
    Grandma Moses, Archive Photos; page 60, Isamu Noguchi, *Capital* (1939),
    Georgia marble, 16" x 24" x 24", The Museum of Modern Art, New York,
    gift of Miss Jeanne Reynal, photograph © 1997, The Museum of Modern
    Art, New York; page 60, Frank Lloyd Wright house, Archive Photos;
    page 60, Georgia O'Keeffe, *Oriental Poppies,* 1928, oil on canvas, H 30"
    x W 40⅛", collection Frederick R. Weisman Art Museum, University of
    Minnesota, Minneapolis; page 61, Emily Dickinson, Amherst College
    Library, by permission of the Trustees of Amherst College; pages 61
    and 63, Langston Hughes, Archive Photos; page 61, Maya Angelou, Nancy
    Kaszerman/Shooting Star; page 61, Mark Twain, Stock Montage, Inc.;
    pages 61 and 69, Ella Fitzgerald, SS Archive/Shooting Star; page 61,
    Steven Spielberg, Spike Nannarello/Shooting Star; page 61, Louis
    Armstrong, Roy Avery/Shooting Star; page 61, Katharine Hepburn, Michael
    Montfort/Shooting Star; page 72, etching of slave auction, Corbis-
    Bettmann; page 78, John Brown, Stock Montage, Inc.; page 81, Sitting Bull,
    Stock Montage, Inc.

Editorial director: Joanne Dresner
Senior acquisitions editor: Allen Ascher
Associate editor: Jessica Miller
Senior production editor: Linda Moser
Text design adaptation: Inez Sovjani
Cover design: Naomi Ganor
Cover credits: Top row, left to right: © National Air & Space Museum,
    Smithsonian Institution, Photo No. A 26767 B-2; Jill Wood, Woodshed
    Productions; Stock Montage, Inc. Center row, left to right: Jill Wood,
    Woodshed Productions; Stock Montage, Inc.; Jill Wood, Woodshed
    Productions. Bottom row, left to right: Roy Avery/Shooting Star; Jill Wood,
    Woodshed Productions; McDonald's Corporation
Text art: Jill Wood/Woodshed Productions, except for page 13, old
    telephone, Pencil Point Studio; page 24, Coke bottle, Pencil Point Studio;
    page 24, man in tuxedo, Laura Hartman Maestro; page 25, chewing gum,
    Pencil Point Studio; page 29, hamburger, Pencil Point Studio; page 37,
    jack-o'-lantern, Laura Hartman Maestro
Photo research: Amy Durfy

Library of Congress Cataloging-in-Publication Data

Broukal, Milada.
    A first look at the USA : a cultural reader / Milada Broukal.
        p. cm.
    ISBN 0-201-69512-X
    1. Readers—United States.   2. United States—Civilization—Problems,
exercises, etc.   3. English language—Textbooks for foreign speakers.
I. Title.
PE1127.H5B685   1997
    428.6'4—dc21   96-48752
                                                        CIP

ISBN: 0-201-69512-X

1 2 3 4 5 6 7 8 9 10–CRS–00999897

CONTENTS

INTRODUCTION

A First Look at the USA is a beginning reader for students of English as a Second Language. Its seven parts introduce general-knowledge topics about the United States such as U.S. Inventions and Inventors, Holidays and Special Days, and the Story of America. Three chapter readings elaborate on specific topics in each part. The readings are primarily written in the present tense, and the vocabulary and structures have been carefully controlled at a beginning level, while every effort has been made to keep the language natural.

Each part consists of an illustrated presentation of the general knowledge area, a "quiz" on the general knowledge area, and three units, each based on a short reading passage related to the part theme. Each unit contains:

- Prereading questions and introductory visuals
- Topic-related vocabulary work
- Comprehension and Looking for Details
- Activity
- Writing

The prereading questions are linked to the visual on the first page of each unit. They focus the student on the topic of the unit by introducing names, encouraging speculation about content, relating the topic to the students' own experience when possible, and presenting vocabulary as the need arises.

The reading of each passage should, ideally, first be done individually by skimming for a general feel for content. The teacher may wish to deal with some of the vocabulary at this point. A second, more detailed individual reading could be done while working through the vocabulary exercise. Further reading(s) could be done aloud with the teacher or with the class.

The VOCABULARY exercise is designed to help students become more self-reliant by encouraging them to work out the meaning from context. As in all exercise sections, a variety of exercise types is used.

There are two COMPREHENSION exercises: In the first one students are asked to confirm the basic content of the text. This takes a variety of forms, such as *Understanding the Main Idea* and *Following the Sequence*. This exercise should be used in conjunction with the text to help students develop their reading skills, and not as a test of memory. Students can do this exercise individually, in pairs, in small groups, or as a class. The second exercise, *Looking for Details,* expands the students' exploration of the text, concentrating on the skimming and scanning skills necessary to derive maximum value from reading.

ACTIVITY personalizes a theme related to the reading, encouraging students to share their own ideas or knowledge with their classmates.

WRITING provides the stimulus for students to write simple sentences. Teachers should use their own judgment when deciding whether or not to correct the Writing exercises.

Part 1

THE UNITED STATES

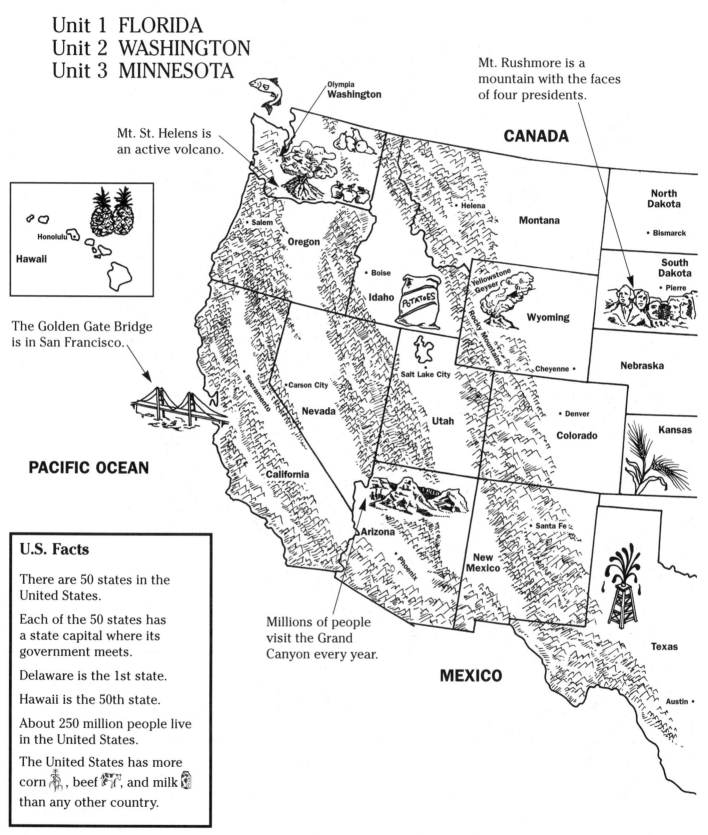

Mt. St. Helens is an active volcano.

Mt. Rushmore is a mountain with the faces of four presidents.

The Golden Gate Bridge is in San Francisco.

Millions of people visit the Grand Canyon every year.

PACIFIC OCEAN

CANADA

MEXICO

Hawaii

Honolulu

Washington
Olympia
Salem
Oregon
Boise
Idaho
Carson City
Nevada
Sacramento
California
Arizona
Phoenix
Helena
Montana
Salt Lake City
Utah
Yellowstone Geyser
Wyoming
Rocky Mountains
Cheyenne
Colorado
Denver
Santa Fe
New Mexico
North Dakota
Bismarck
South Dakota
Pierre
Nebraska
Kansas
Texas
Austin

U.S. Facts

There are 50 states in the United States.

Each of the 50 states has a state capital where its government meets.

Delaware is the 1st state.

Hawaii is the 50th state.

About 250 million people live in the United States.

The United States has more corn, beef, and milk than any other country.

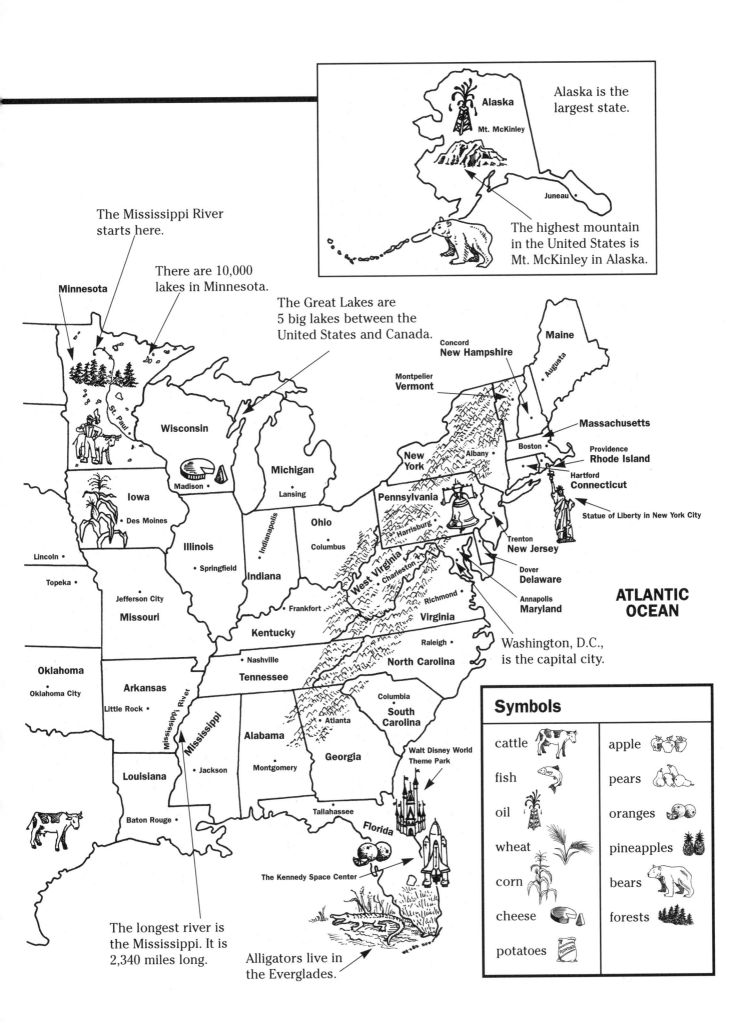

The Mississippi River starts here.

There are 10,000 lakes in Minnesota.

The Great Lakes are 5 big lakes between the United States and Canada.

Alaska is the largest state.

The highest mountain in the United States is Mt. McKinley in Alaska.

Alaska

Mt. McKinley

Juneau

Minnesota

St. Paul

Wisconsin

Madison

Michigan

Lansing

Maine

Augusta

Concord
New Hampshire

Montpelier
Vermont

Massachusetts

Boston

Providence
Rhode Island

Hartford
Connecticut

Statue of Liberty in New York City

New York

Albany

Iowa

Des Moines

Illinois

Springfield

Indianapolis

Indiana

Ohio

Columbus

Pennsylvania

Harrisburg

Trenton
New Jersey

Dover
Delaware

Annapolis
Maryland

Washington, D.C., is the capital city.

ATLANTIC OCEAN

Lincoln

Topeka

Jefferson City

Missouri

Frankfort

Kentucky

Nashville

West Virginia

Charleston

Richmond

Virginia

Raleigh

North Carolina

Oklahoma

Oklahoma City

Arkansas

Little Rock

Tennessee

Mississippi River

Mississippi

Alabama

Montgomery

Georgia

Atlanta

Columbia
South Carolina

Walt Disney World Theme Park

Louisiana

Jackson

Baton Rouge

Tallahassee

Florida

The Kennedy Space Center

The longest river is the Mississippi. It is 2,340 miles long.

Alligators live in the Everglades.

Symbols

cattle	apple
fish	pears
oil	oranges
wheat	pineapples
corn	bears
cheese	forests
potatoes	

Quiz

Fill in the blanks with the information from the map from *The United States*.

1. There are _____ states in the United States.

2. About _____ million people live in the United States.

3. _____ is the capital city of the United States.

4. _____ is the largest state.

5. The longest river is the _____.

6. Olympia is the state capital of _____.

7. The Mississippi River starts in _____.

8. The Grand Canyon is in _____.

9. The highest mountain is in _____.

10. Hawaii is in the _____ Ocean.

11. _____ is the first state.

12. The Golden Gate Bridge is in the state of _____.

13. Mount Rushmore is in _____ _____.

14. There are 10,000 lakes in _____.

15. The Kennedy Space Center is in _____.

16. _____ is the 50th state.

17. Oranges grow in _____.

18. Corn grows in _____.

19. The United States has more _____, _____, and
    _____ than any other country.

20. Austin is in _____.

21. Bears live in _____.

22. Potatoes grow in _____.

23. Texas has cattle and _____.

24. Cheese comes from _____.

25. Pineapples grow in _____.

FLORIDA

Why do people like to live in a warm place?
Why do you think tourists like to go to Florida?
What do you know about Disney World?

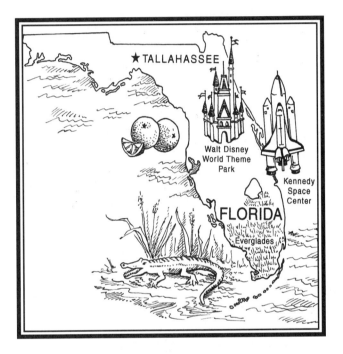

Welcome to Florida, the "Sunshine State." If you like warm weather, Florida is the best place for a vacation. Millions of visitors come to Florida each year. They like its sandy beaches, theme parks, and natural beauty.

Miami is a big tourist city. People love its beautiful beaches. There are many coconut palm trees along the streets and beaches in Miami. They are very pretty. But they are also dangerous! People have jobs as coconut watchers. They make sure that coconuts do not fall on the tourists' heads!

Florida is famous for its theme parks. The world's largest theme park is Walt Disney World, near Orlando. A train takes people around Disney World. One part, called EPCOT Center, is all about the future. You can see life, food, and transportation in the future.

Florida has other things to see, too. You can go to the Kennedy Space Center. This is where flights go up into space with astronauts in them. You can see how they teach astronauts. If you go south, you can see wildlife in the Everglades. The Everglades is an area of some land and a lot of water. Grass grows in the water. Many wild animals such as alligators live in this swamp.

Millions of tourists come to Florida for a vacation. But many people come to Florida to live, too. Many older people from cold states come to relax in the Florida sunshine. But young people come to Florida, too. Florida has many new kinds of jobs. Florida has something for everyone.

VOCABULARY

Match the words and the pictures. Write your answer on the line.

astronauts	swamp	palm trees
theme park	alligator	

1. ___swamp___

2. _____

3. _____

4. _____

5. _____

COMPREHENSION

Understanding the Main Idea

Circle the letter of the best answer.

1. People like to visit Florida because
   a. there are many things to see and do.
   b. there are many jobs for young people.
   c. visitors can learn how to become astronauts.

2. Many older people live in Florida because
   a. there are theme parks to visit.
   b. the weather is warm.
   c. there are many kinds of fruits to eat.

Looking for Details

Complete each sentence with the correct word or words. Write the letter of your answer on the line.

1. Florida is famous for its ___g___ .

2. Florida is called the "Sunshine State" because of its ____ .

3. The EPCOT Center is all about the ____ .

4. At the Kennedy Space Center, you can see how they teach ____ .

5. There are ____ in the Everglades.

6. Many older people go to Florida to ____ .

7. Many ____ grow along the streets in Miami.

a. astronauts

b. relax

c. future

d. warm weather

e. coconut palm trees

f. alligators

g. theme parks

ACTIVITY

What do you like to see and do on vacation? Place an X beside the things you like.

____ Sunbathe by a pool

____ Go to a theme park

____ Travel in a car

____ See a famous city

____ Go camping

____ See famous buildings

____ Go shopping

____ Stay in expensive hotels

____ Travel in a tour bus

____ See a place of natural beauty

Compare answers with your classmates. What do most of the students like to do on vacation?

WRITING

Write five sentences. Say where you like to go on vacation and the things you like to do there.

EXAMPLE: _I like to go to Florida. I like to go to the beach._

1. _____

2. _____

3. _____

4. _____

5. _____

WASHINGTON

Which is better—a lot of rain or a lot of sun? Why?

What can you do in a place with mountains, rivers, and forests?

Why do people move to a new state?

Why is Washington different from every other state in the United States? It is the only state named after a president. Washington is named after the first president of the United States, George Washington. It is a beautiful state. It is called the "Evergreen State." Washington is very green because it rains a lot there.

The rain helps many things grow. There are trees and forests everywhere. People cut down the trees for wood. But they plant a new tree for each tree that they cut down. So Washington has beautiful forests. There are also many fruit trees. Washington is number one in the United States for apples and pears.

Washington has many mountains and rivers. There are 40 kinds of fish in the rivers. But Washington is most famous for its salmon. Washington also has a lot of volcanoes. In 1980 the volcano at Mount St. Helens erupted. The smoke from the mountain turned the day into night. Trees and plants died. Sixty people near Mount St. Helens died. But today new life is back on the mountain. Scientists are very surprised that animals and plants are back so soon.

There are over 4 million people in Washington. Many people go there to visit. Some like it so much that they decide to stay. More and more people come to live in this beautiful state.

VOCABULARY

Match the words and the pictures. Write your answer on the line.

erupted	forest	smoke
cut down	volcanoes	salmon

1. _____smoke_____   2. _____   3. _____

4. _____   5. _____   6. _____

COMPREHENSION

Past and Present

What is the past tense of the verb? Draw a line to it.

1. name   turned

2. call   died

3. erupt   called

4. turn   named

5. die   erupted

Looking for Details

Circle T if the sentence is true. Circle F if it is false.

		True	False
1.	There are many states named after a U.S. president.	T	(F)
2.	There are not many trees in Washington.	T	F
3.	Washington is famous for its oranges.	T	F
4.	Washington has many mountains and rivers.	T	F
5.	Mount St. Helens erupted in 1990.	T	F
6.	Sixty people died when the volcano erupted.	T	F

ACTIVITY

Which outdoor sports do you like to do? Talk with a partner.

skiing	rock climbing	rafting	hiking
bicycling	camping	fishing	

Compare answers with your classmates. Which sport do people like most? Least? Why?

WRITING

Imagine you are lost in a forest. Write a sentence to answer each question.

1. What do you eat?

   I eat plants.

2. What do you drink?

   _____

3. Where do you sleep?

   _____

4. What animals do you see?

   _____

5. How do you get home?

   _____

MINNESOTA

What are some ways we use lakes and rivers?

If you live in a cold climate, what problems do you have?

What activities can you do in a cold climate?

Minnesota has many lakes. People call Minnesota the "Land of 10,000 Lakes." In fact, there are more than 15,000 lakes. It also has rivers. The great Mississippi River begins at Lake Itasca. It is very small where it starts. The river then flows 2,340 miles to the Gulf of Mexico.

The name *Minnesota* is a Native American word. Can you guess what it means? If you think that Minnesota means "water," you are right. It means "sky-colored water." It is a good name for this state.

Minnesota also has many forests. People tell a story about a woodcutter named Paul Bunyan. He is very large. They say he cuts down 500 trees before breakfast.

Minnesota is beautiful, but it is very cold in the winter. In the biggest city, Minneapolis, there are skyways between many buildings. Skyways are like bridges. With the skyways, people walk from place to place without going out into the cold.

St. Paul is the capital of Minnesota. Here, at the winter carnival, people make ice sculptures.

Minnesota is a safe and healthy place to live. It has the best school system in the country. Students choose the school they want to go to. The medical system is also very good.

VOCABULARY

Write the correct word in the blanks.

sculptures	woodcutter	skyways
flows	carnival	

1. People make ice sculptures at the winter _____carnival_____ in St. Paul.

2. Paul Bunyan is a _____. He cuts down trees.

3. The people in Minneapolis do not like to walk outside during the winter. So they use

   _____ to walk from place to place.

4. The Mississippi River is the greatest river in the United States. It _____ all
   the way from Minnesota to the Gulf of Mexico.

5. During the winter, the people of Minnesota use ice to make _____ of people
   and objects.

COMPREHENSION

Using Pronouns

Write the letter of the answer that matches the underlined pronoun.

1. Can you guess what <u>it</u> means? _d_   **a.** the state of Minnesota

2. <u>It</u> also has rivers. ____   **b.** Paul Bunyan

3. <u>It</u> is very small where it starts. ____   **c.** the Mississippi River

4. <u>They</u> say he cuts down 500 trees before breakfast. ____   **d.** the name *Minnesota*

5. They say <u>he</u> cuts down 500 trees before breakfast. ____   **e.** people

Looking for Details

Which sentence is correct? Circle *a* or *b*.

1. **a.** The name *Minnesota* means "10,000 lakes."
   b. The name *Minnesota* means "sky-colored water."

2. **a.** The Mississippi River is very large at its beginning.
   b. The Mississippi River is not large at all at its beginning.

3. **a.** Skyways help people in Minneapolis travel from place to place very quickly.
   b. Skyways help people in Minneapolis get from place to place without going out into
      the cold.

4. a. Minnesota has a good school system.

b. Minnesota does not have a good school system.

5. a. The capital of Minnesota is St. Paul.

b. The capital of Minnesota is Minneapolis.

ACTIVITY

Think of the best place to live. What is it like? Use some of these words.

forests	lakes	rivers	deserts
mountains	many people	few people	beaches

Compare answers with your classmates. What kind of place do people like most? Least? Why?

WRITING

Write five sentences. Tell about the most perfect place you can think of.

EXAMPLE: _There are trees and lakes._ _____

1. _____

2. _____

3. _____

4. _____

5. _____

Part 2

U.S. INVENTIONS AND INVENTORS

Unit 4 ISAAC SINGER'S SEWING MACHINE
Unit 5 JOSEPHINE COCHRANE'S DISHWASHER
Unit 6 GARRET A. MORGAN'S TRAFFIC LIGHT

INVENTIONS THAT ENTERTAIN US

Phonograph
Thomas Edison invents the phonograph in **1877**.

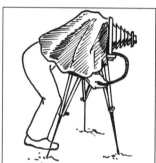

Kodak Camera
George Eastman produces the Kodak camera in **1888**.

Television
Vladimir Zworykin invents television in **1924**.

Sewing Machine
In **1851** Isaac Singer makes a sewing machine that works well. In **1886** he starts the I. M. Singer Company.

INVENTIONS THAT MAKE LIFE EASIER

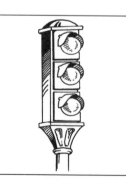

Traffic Light
Garret A. Morgan invents the traffic light in **1916**.

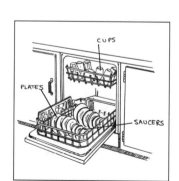

Dishwasher
Josephine Cochrane invents the dishwasher in **1886**.

INVENTIONS THAT TAKE US FROM PLACE TO PLACE

Gasoline Automobile
Charles Duryea and J. Frank Duryea invent the first gasoline automobile in **1892**.

Motor Airplane
Orville and Wilbur Wright fly in their motor airplane in **1903**.

Helicopter
Igor Sikorsky builds the helicopter in **1939**.

INVENTIONS THAT HELP OUR HEALTH

Bifocal Lenses for Eyeglasses
Benjamin Franklin invents bifocal lenses for eyeglasses in **1780**.

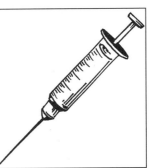

Polio Vaccine
Jonas Salk develops the polio vaccine in **1955**.

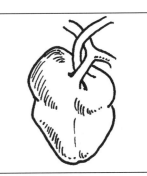

Artificial Heart
Robert Jarvik makes the artificial heart in **1982**.

INVENTIONS THAT HELP US COMMUNICATE WITH EACH OTHER

Telegraph
Samuel Morse invents the telegraph in **1837**.

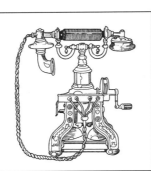

Telephone
Alexander Graham Bell invents the telephone in **1876**.

Xerox Copies
Chester Carlson invents a machine to make Xerox copies in **1938**.

Quiz

Fill in the blanks with the information from _U.S. Inventions and Inventors_.

1. Samuel Morse invents the _____ in 1837.

2. _____ _____ develops the polio vaccine in 1955.

3. Orville and Wilbur Wright invent the first motor airplane in _____ .

4. Vladimir Zworykin invents _____ in 1924.

5. _____ _____ invents the phonograph in 1877.

6. Josephine Cochrane invents the _____ in 1886.

7. Igor Sikorsky invents the _____ in 1939.

8. Alexander Graham Bell invents the _____ in 1876.

9. In 1780 _____ _____ invents bifocal lenses for eyeglasses.

10. Charles and J. Frank Duryea invent the first gasoline automobile in _____ .

11. Garret A. Morgan invents the _____ _____ in 1916.

12. Chester Carlson invents Xerox copies in _____ .

13. George Eastman invents the _____ camera in 1888.

14. In 1982 _____ _____ invents the artificial heart.

15. Isaac Singer invents the _____ _____ in 1851.

ISAAC SINGER'S SEWING MACHINE

What can you make with a sewing machine?

How long do you think it takes to make a shirt with no sewing machine?

How does the sewing machine help people?

Imagine life with no machines. Make your own shoes. Sew your own clothes. Wash clothes by hand. Walk everywhere. Life is very hard! Modern people have a very easy life. But that is not because of machines. It is because of inventors.

Like many inventors, Isaac Singer begins life poor. He is the eighth child of a German immigrant. At age 12, he runs away from home and becomes an actor. An actor does not make much money, so Isaac also learns to be a mechanic. When he needs money, he works as a mechanic.

It is 1851. Singer is working as a mechanic in Boston. Someone tells him he can make a lot of money if he can make a good sewing machine. Singer needs money. There are already several kinds of sewing machines. But none of them work well. In eleven days, Singer makes the first sewing machine that really works.

Singer and two other people start the I. M. Singer Company. They make sewing machines. Soon everyone wants to buy one. The Singer Company uses a great new idea to sell its machines. People do not have to pay all the money at one time. They can pay a little money every month or every week.

The sewing machine changes life in the United States. Women do not have to sew clothes for the family. For the first time, people can buy ready-made clothes and shoes.

Isaac Singer is a very, very wealthy man. He stops work and retires. He builds a house with 115 rooms in England. When he dies, his 24 children fight over his money.

VOCABULARY

Write the opposites. You can find the words in the story.

1. a little   <u>a</u>   <u>l</u>   <u>o</u>   <u>t</u>

2. teaches   ___ ___ ___ ___ <u>n</u> ___

3. all   ___ <u>o</u> ___ ___

4. stop   ___ <u>t</u> ___ ___ ___

5. sell   ___ ___ <u>y</u>

6. hand-made   <u>r</u> ___ ___ ___ ___ - ___ ___ ___ <u>e</u>

7. poor   ___ <u>e</u> ___ ___ ___ ___ <u>y</u>

8. starts work   <u>r</u> ___ ___ ___ ___ <u>e</u> ___

COMPREHENSION

Understanding the Main Idea

Circle the letter of the best answer.

1. Singer wants to make a good sewing machine because
   a. he needs a good sewing machine.
   b. he needs money.
   c. he likes to be a good mechanic.

2. People want to buy from the I. M. Singer Company because
   a. they like Isaac Singer.
   b. the Singer Company has many kinds of sewing machines.
   c. they do not have to pay all the money at one time.

Looking for Details

One word in each sentence is *not* correct. Find the word and cross it out. Write the correct word.

1. Isaac Singer runs away from home to become an ~~immigrant~~. *actor*

2. In eight days, Singer makes a sewing machine that works.

3. In 1851, Singer and three other people start the I. M. Singer Company.

4. The Singer Company uses a great new idea to buy its machines.

5. Singer builds a house with 115 rooms in France.

ACTIVITY

Imagine you are very wealthy. What do you want to do? Mark *two* things with an *X*. On the last line, write one *other* thing you want to do.

1. Travel   _____

2. Buy a very big house   _____

3. Buy a boat   _____

4. Buy a house for your parents   _____

5. Give the money to the poor or sick   _____

6. Other   _____

In a small group, show your answers to your classmates. Are your answers the same? Which things have the most *X's*? What is the most interesting answer for line 6?

WRITING

Write five sentences about what you do not want to do when you are very wealthy.

EXAMPLE: _I don't want to clean my home._

1. _____

2. _____

3. _____

4. _____

5. _____

JOSEPHINE COCHRANE'S DISHWASHER

What do you put in a dishwasher?

Why do people use a dishwasher?

Do you use a dishwasher or wash dishes by hand?
Which do you like better?

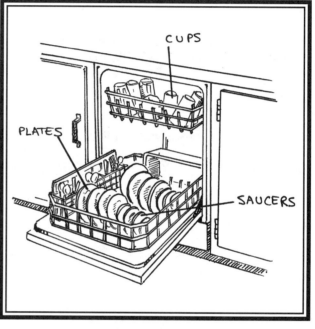

Josephine Cochrane is a very rich woman. She has many beautiful things. She never washes dishes or does housework. She has servants to do the work for her. Mrs. Cochrane has a very good life. But Mrs. Cochrane is not happy! Why? Her servants always break her lovely dishes. One day another dish breaks. Mrs. Cochrane gets angry. She decides to do something. She decides to make a machine that washes dishes.

Mrs. Cochrane does not know anything about machines. So she asks her friends for help. Finally she makes a dishwasher. It has places for plates, saucers, and cups. It is a lot like dishwashers today. She makes the machine and shows it to her friends. Her friends think the machine is amazing. They tell other friends. Soon many people know about Mrs. Cochrane's machine. Restaurants and hotels want to have a machine. In 1886 Mrs. Cochrane starts a company to make dishwashers.

Later, her company makes the first dishwashers for the home. She names her dishwasher *Kitchen-Aid*. Today, half the homes in the United States have dishwashers. Many people still buy Kitchen-Aid dishwashers. Everyone can thank Mrs. Cochrane for saving their nice dishes.

VOCABULARY

Write the correct word in the blanks.

servants	saucers	company
lovely	amazing	break

1. Mrs. Cochrane's friends see her dishwasher. They are very surprised. They think it is
   amazing .

2. Mrs. Cochrane likes to have tea parties. She wants to serve her tea in beautiful cups
   and _____ .

3. Josephine Cochrane starts her own _____ . The people who work there make dishwashers.

4. Mrs. Cochrane has _____ to do all her housework for her.

5. Mrs. Cochrane's dishes are very pretty. She tells the servants to be careful with her
   _____ dishes.

6. Sometimes the servants drop Mrs. Cochrane's dishes and they _____ .

COMPREHENSION

Following the Sequence

Which happens first? Write 1 on the line. Which happens next? Write 2 on the line.

1. __2__ Mrs. Cochrane decides to make a dishwashing machine.

   __1__ Mrs. Cochrane's servants break her dishes.

2. ____ Mrs. Cochrane makes a dishwasher.

   ____ Mrs. Cochrane asks her friends for help.

3. ____ Mrs. Cochrane's friends think the machine is amazing.

   ____ Mrs. Cochrane shows the machine to her friends.

4. ____ Restaurants and hotels want to have Mrs. Cochrane's dishwasher.

   ____ Mrs. Cochrane's friends talk to people about the machine.

5. ____ Mrs. Cochrane starts a company.

   ____ Mrs. Cochrane's company makes dishwashers for the home.

Looking for Details

Which sentence is correct? Circle *a* or *b*.

1. **(a.)** Mrs. Cochrane never washes dishes.
   b. Mrs. Cochrane always washes dishes.

2. **a.** Mrs. Cochrane makes a dishwasher.
   b. Mrs. Cochrane's friends make a dishwasher.

3. **a.** Mrs. Cochrane shows the machine to her friends.
   b. Mrs. Cochrane shows the machine to hotels.

4. **a.** In 1886 Mrs. Cochrane makes dishwashers for the home.
   b. In 1886 Mrs. Cochrane starts a company.

ACTIVITY

What machines do you use? What machines do you want?

EXAMPLE: I use a vacuum cleaner. I want a dishwasher.

dishwasher	microwave oven	washing machine
vacuum cleaner	toaster	

Share your answers with your classmates. Are your answers the same?

WRITING

Look at the pictures below. Make sentences with the words under the pictures. Write your sentences on the lines.

1. Mrs. Cochrane's servants/break/dishes

2. Mrs. Cochrane/get/angry

3. Mrs. Cochrane/make/dishwasher

4. 1886/Mrs. Cochrane/start/company

1. _____Mrs. Cochrane's servants break her dishes._____

2. _____

3. _____

4. _____

GARRET A. MORGAN'S TRAFFIC LIGHT

What inventions make life easier and safer?

What is your favorite invention? Why?

Imagine you can invent a machine. What does it do?

Think about driving without traffic lights. What a nightmare! The next time you stop for a red light, thank the inventor, Garret A. Morgan.

Garret A. Morgan is born in 1875. He is from a poor African-American family. When he is 14 he leaves school and goes to work. He does not have much education. But he is very imaginative. He teaches himself.

Morgan works in a sewing machine shop. He gets interested in machines. He always looks for better ways to do things. In 1901 he invents a special belt for sewing machines. He sells the idea for $150. But this is only the beginning. Morgan invents many things. In 1914, he invents a helmet to protect miners and firefighters from smoke and gas. He wins a gold medal for this invention.

Morgan looks for other problems to solve. Cars are very popular in the United States. The streets are crowded with cars. There are many accidents. Morgan has an idea. What about a light at each street corner? The light tells the cars to stop or go. In 1916 he invents a timer that automatically changes the light.

Cities all over the country want to have Morgan's traffic lights. He cannot produce enough traffic lights. He sells his invention to the General Electric Company in the 1920s. He gets $40,000. This is a large amount of money for that time. Morgan is a great success.

VOCABULARY

Write the correct word in the blanks.

timer	helmet	imaginative
produce	nightmare	crowded

1. At first, there are only a few cars on the road. But more and more people drive cars. After a while the roads are ____crowded____ .

2. Garret Morgan cannot make enough traffic lights. But the General Electric Company can _____ many lights.

3. Morgan's street light has a _____ that makes the light change every minute or two.

4. Morgan always has new ideas. He is very _____ .

5. Firefighters put Morgan's special _____ on their heads.

6. Imagine streets without traffic lights. There are many accidents. People are hurt. This idea is a _____ .

COMPREHENSION

Following the Sequence

Which happens first? Write 1 on the line. Which happens next? Write 2 on the line.

1. _2_ Garret A. Morgan goes to work.

   _1_ Garret A. Morgan leaves school.

2. ____ Morgan works in a sewing machine shop.

   ____ Morgan gets interested in machines.

3. ____ Morgan invents a helmet for firefighters.

   ____ Morgan invents a special belt for sewing machines.

4. ____ There are many car accidents.

   ____ The streets are crowded with cars.

5. ____ Morgan invents a traffic light with a timer.

   ____ Morgan sells his invention to the General Electric Company.

Looking for Details

One word in each sentence is **not** correct. Find the word and cross it out. Write the correct word or words.

1875
1. Garret Morgan is born in ~~1975~~.

2. Morgan is from a rich African-American family.

3. In 1901 Morgan invents a helmet.

4. Morgan buys his idea for $150.

5. Morgan wins a gold watch for his helmet invention.

6. Morgan cannot produce enough helmets.

ACTIVITY

Do you think these inventions are good or bad? Why?

computer games	microwave oven	robots
television	spaceships	

Talk with a partner. Which invention does your partner think is good? Which does your partner think is bad? Why?

WRITING

Look at the pictures below. Make sentences with the words under the pictures. Write your sentences on the lines.

1. Morgan/work/ sewing machine shop

2. 1914/Morgan/ invents/helmet/ protect/miners/ firefighters

3. Morgan/has/ idea./What about/ light/each/street corner?

4. Many/cities/want/ Morgan/traffic light

1. ___Morgan works in a sewing machine shop._____

2. _____

3. _____

4. _____

Part 3

U.S. ORIGINALS

Unit 7 McDONALD'S
Unit 8 SUPERMAN
Unit 9 POTATO CHIPS

Potato Chips
George Crum is a chef. He makes very thin french fries in **1853**. Soon everyone wants Crum's special potato chips.

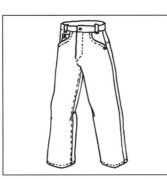

Jeans
Levi Strauss comes to California from Germany. He makes the first jeans in **1860**.

Coca-Cola
Dr. John Pemberton is a druggist. He invents Coca-Cola in **1886** in Atlanta, Georgia.

Tuxedo
Lorillard is a rich man from Tuxedo Park, New York. He gets the idea in **1886**.

Avon
David McConnel is a salesman. He starts Avon cosmetics in **1886**.

Peanut Butter
In **1890**, a doctor in St. Louis first makes peanut butter.

Chewing Gum

William Wrigley makes flavored chewing gum in **1892**.

Gillette

In **1903** King Gillette makes safe blades for razors.

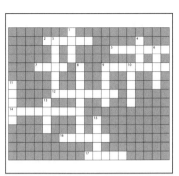

Crossword Puzzle

Arthur Wayne makes the first crossword puzzle. It is in the newspaper for the first time in **1913**.

Corn Flakes

W. W. Kellogg starts the Kellogg Company in **1922**. He makes Corn Flakes.

Reader's Digest

Mr. and Mrs. Wallace start the magazine in **1922**.

Xerox

Chester Carlson invents the photocopy machine in **1938**.

Superman

Jerry Siegel and Joe Shuster make the story of Superman in **1939**.

McDonald's

Two brothers open a restaurant. In **1961** the brothers sell McDonald's. They get $2.5 million.

Federal Express

Frederick Smith is a pilot. He can deliver mail in one day. He starts a company in **1973**.

Quiz

Fill in the blanks with the information from *U.S. Originals*.

1. Levi _____ makes the first jeans.

2. A pilot starts _____ _____ in 1973.

3. Mr. and Mrs. Wallace start the magazine _____ _____ in 1922.

4. A druggist invents _____ _____ in Atlanta, Georgia.

5. William _____ makes flavored chewing gum.

6. W. W. Kellogg makes _____ _____ in 1922.

7. A doctor in St. Louis makes _____ _____ .

8. The tuxedo gets it name from _____ _____ , New York.

9. King _____ makes razors safe.

10. A salesman starts _____ cosmetics.

11. A chef makes his french fries very thin, and soon everyone wants his _____

    _____ .

12. Jerry Siegel and Joe Shuster make the story of _____ in 1939.

13. _____ , a machine for photocopying, comes out in 1938.

14. Arthur Wayne makes the first _____ _____ for a newspaper in 1913.

15. Two brothers start the restaurant _____ .

McDONALD'S

Why is fast food so popular?

What is your favorite fast food?

How many fast-food restaurants can you name?

Do you have a dream? What do you want to do?

Maurice ("Mac") and Richard McDonald have a dream. They want to be movie stars. They go to California from the East Coast. But they cannot find jobs in the movies. They are very poor. They are very disappointed. They must do something to make money. They decide to open a restaurant in San Bernardino. They want to try something new—a fast-food restaurant. They borrow money and open a restaurant. They call the restaurant McDonald's. Hamburgers, milk shakes, and french fries are on the menu. That's all. A restaurant with three things on the menu? No one thinks it will work. But people love it. The food is simple, fast, and good. Soon, people wait in line outside the restaurant.

A salesman named Ray Kroc in Chicago cannot understand why the restaurant wants so many milk-shake machines. So he goes to California to see this restaurant. He is amazed. People wait outside the restaurant to get in. He tries the food. It is great. And the restaurant is so clean.

Kroc asks the brothers to open other restaurants like this. The brothers say they make enough money. Kroc tells the brothers they can make more money. He can open other McDonald's like this one. He will give them some money from these restaurants. The brothers agree.

In 1955 Kroc opens two other McDonald's. But people want more. By 1961 there are 300 McDonald's. The brothers have enough money. They sell McDonald's to Ray Kroc. He pays $2.5 million.

Kroc becomes very rich. And the brothers? They are happy with their quiet life.

VOCABULARY

Write the correct word in the blanks.

disappointed	dream	borrow
enough	milk shakes	

1. Mac and Richard McDonald have a _____dream_____. They want to be movie stars.

2. The McDonald brothers do not have any money to open the restaurant. They must _____ from someone.

3. Mac and Richard want to be movie stars. But they cannot find jobs. They feel sad. They are _____ .

4. Mac and Richard make a lot of _____ . They use milk, ice, and sugar.

5. Mac and Richard do not need more money. They have _____ .

COMPREHENSION

Following the Sequence

Which happens first? Write 1 on the line. Which happens next? Write 2 on the line.

1. __1__ Mac and Richard go to California. They want to be movie stars.
   __2__ Mac and Richard cannot find jobs in the movies.

2. ____ The McDonald brothers open a fast-food restaurant.
   ____ The McDonald brothers borrow money.

3. ____ People wait in line to get into McDonald's.
   ____ Mac and Richard try a simple menu—hamburgers, milk shakes, and french fries.

4. ____ Kroc thinks McDonald's is a great restaurant.
   ____ Kroc goes to California.

5. ____ Kroc tells the brothers they can make more money.
   ____ Kroc opens two more McDonald's restaurants.

6. ____ Mac and Richard sell McDonald's to Ray Kroc. He pays $2.5 million.
   ____ Kroc becomes very rich.

Looking for Details

One word in each sentence is **not** correct. Find the word and cross it out. Write the correct word or words.

1. Mac and Richard McDonald go to California from the ~~West~~ <u>East</u> Coast.

2. Hamburgers, salads, and milk shakes are on the first McDonald's menu.

3. Ray Kroc is a salesman from Boston.

4. Ray Kroc thinks the service is great at McDonald's.

5. Kroc opens five other McDonald's in 1955.

6. The brothers are unhappy with their quiet life.

ACTIVITY

Imagine you are one of the McDonald brothers. Do you want to sell your restaurant? Give three reasons.

EXAMPLE: _____ I want to be rich. _____

1. _____

2. _____

3. _____

Compare answers with your classmates. What are their reasons?

WRITING

Look at the pictures below. Make sentences with the words under the pictures. Write your sentences on the lines.

1. Mac and Richard McDonald/open/ fast-food restaurant

2. People/wait/ line/outside/ restaurant

3. Ray Kroc/go/ California/see/ McDonald's

4. Brothers/sell/ McDonald's/ Ray Kroc

1. _____ Mac and Richard McDonald open a fast food restaurant. _____

2. _____

3. _____

4. _____

SUPERMAN

Why do so many people like Superman?

*Do you like to read books about heroes? Do you like
to see movies?*

Do you have any real-life heroes?

"Look, up in the sky. It's a bird! It's a plane! It's Superman!" Everyone knows Superman. Old people know Superman. Young people know Superman. He is famous. Millions of people buy Superman comic books.

The story of Superman begins in 1939. Jerry Siegel and Joe Shuster are high school students. Jerry wants to be a writer. Joe wants to be an artist. They like to work together. One writes. The other draws pictures. They write stories with pictures for comic books.

One day, Jerry gets a great new idea. It is Superman! Superman is from another planet. But nobody knows. He lives like an ordinary person. Superman does good things for people. Joe draws Superman. They want to sell their great idea. They want to make money. But nobody buys Superman. Finally, after many years, someone wants to buy Superman. Jerry and Joe are very excited. But they sell Superman for only a little money.

Superman is a great success. The people who own Superman now make millions of dollars. But Joe and Jerry are poor. Joe cannot see well now. He cannot draw. He lives in a poor apartment. Jerry works for very little money. He is poor, too.

It is 1975. The two men are both old and poor. They are angry, too. They tell the newspapers about their situation. Finally, the owners of Superman give Joe and Jerry some money. The money helps the old men. But it is still not much. Other people make a lot more money from Superman. It is also 30 years too late. Superman is famous. His owners are rich. But Joe and Jerry are not so lucky.

VOCABULARY

Write the correct word or words in the blanks.

planet	hero	ordinary	artist
comic books	lucky	situation	

1. Joe draws pictures. He is an ____artist____ .

2. Superman is not born on earth. He is from a different _____ in space.

3. The people who buy Superman from Jerry and Joe become rich. But good things do not happen to Jerry and Joe. They are not _____ .

4. Jerry and Joe are old and poor. They do not make money from their famous idea. But others get rich. Jerry and Joe are in a bad _____ .

5. Superman helps people. He does good things for them. He is a _____ .

6. Superman has a job. He does things that most people do. He lives an _____ life when he is not a hero.

7. Jerry and Joe write stories with pictures when they are in high school. They like to make _____ .

COMPREHENSION

Matching

Find the best answer to complete the sentence. Write the letter of your answer on the line.

1. Jerry wants to be a writer. Joe wants to be an __e__ .

2. People like Superman because ____ .

3. Superman is a big success, but Jerry and Joe are not happy because ____ .

4. Jerry and Joe tell their story to the newspapers because ____ .

5. The owners of Superman finally give Joe and Jerry some ____ .

a. he is a hero and he helps people

b. they want people to know about their situation

c. money

d. they are poor

e. artist

Looking for Details

Circle T if the sentence is true. Circle F if it is false.

		True	False
1.	Jerry and Joe work well together.	(T)	F
2.	Joe has the idea for Superman.	T	F
3.	Superman helps people.	T	F
4.	Jerry and Joe sell their Superman idea for a lot of money.	T	F
5.	Jerry and Joe are angry when they sell Superman.	T	F
6.	The people who own Superman make millions of dollars.	T	F
7.	Joe and Jerry are very old when they get some more money.	T	F

ACTIVITY

Work with a partner. Discuss this situation: Two men rob a bank. They lock the people in a small room. There is not much air in the room. The robbers are driving away in a fast car.

1. What should Superman do?

2. How can Superman save the people *and* catch the robbers?

3. What should the people in the room do?

Discuss answers with your classmates. Are any ideas the same? Who has the best ideas?

WRITING

Write five sentences about heroes.

EXAMPLE: _A hero saves people._ _____

1. _____

2. _____

3. _____

4. _____

5. _____

POTATO CHIPS

Do you eat potatoes? What is your favorite way to eat them?

What is your favorite snack food?

What things make cooking easier today?

Potato chips are America's favorite snack. Where do potato chips come from?

A Native American named George Crum makes the first potato chips. It is 1853. Crum is a chef in an expensive restaurant in Saratoga Springs, New York. One day, a customer does not like his french fries. He says they are too thick. So Crum makes more, this time thinner. The customer still does not like them. Crum gets mad. He decides to make the customer angry. So he cuts the fries very, very thin. The customer loves them.

Other people want Crum's potato chips. They are a new food on the menu—Saratoga chips. Soon Crum sells the chips in many northern states. Crum opens his own restaurant with his special chips.

Until 1920, people peel potatoes by hand. Then comes the automatic potato peeler. It changes everything. It is faster and easier to make potato chips. Now potato chips are not a specialty. They are a popular snack food—everyone eats them.

Potato chips are popular only in the North. Then a salesman named Herman Lay brings potato chips to the South. He sells potato chips in bags. His business grows. In 1961 Lay's potato chips are famous. Today, Americans eat a lot of potato chips. Americans spend $10.5 million on potato chips every day!

VOCABULARY

Draw a line to connect the words that go together.

1. eating tool   potato chips

2. job   north

3. snack food   automatic peeler

4. state   chef

5. vegetable   menu

6. feeling   fork

7. direction   New York

8. list of food   potato

9. machine   mad

COMPREHENSION

Understanding the Main Idea

Circle the letter of the best answer.

1. Crum makes potato chips because
   a. he wants to try something new.
   b. a customer does not like his french fries.
   c. he wants to open his own restaurant.

2. The automatic peeler makes potato chips a popular snack food because
   a. the chips taste better.
   b. the chips look nicer.
   c. it is easier to make more chips.

Looking for Details

Which sentence is correct? Circle *a* or *b*.

1. **a.** George Crum works as a chef in a restaurant.
   b. George Crum is a customer in a restaurant.

2. **a.** The first time George Crum makes potato chips, he is happy.
   b. The first time George Crum makes potato chips, he is mad.

3. **a.** The customer says his french fries are too thin.
   b. The customer says his french fries are too thick.

4. a. Crum sells his chips only in the North.

   b. Crum sells his chips everywhere.

5. a. George Crum and Herman Lay work together.

   b. Herman Lay starts his own business.

ACTIVITY

What are your classmates' favorite snack foods and drinks? Fill in the chart.

NAME	FAVORITE SNACK	FAVORITE DRINK
Miguel	popcorn	cola

Compare answers with your classmates. Which is the most popular snack? Which is the most popular drink?

WRITING

What food do you know how to cook? How do you cook it?

EXAMPLE: Fried potatoes

First, wash and cut the potatoes.

First, _____

Second, _____

Third, _____

Then, _____

Finally, _____

Part 4

HOLIDAYS AND SPECIAL DAYS

Unit 10 NEW YEAR'S DAY
Unit 11 ST. PATRICK'S DAY
Unit 12 LABOR DAY

JANUARY

New Year's Day
New Year's Day is January 1. Many people watch the Rose Bowl football game on television.

Chinese New Year
Chinese-Americans celebrate the new year in January or February.

Martin Luther King, Jr., Day
On Martin Luther King, Jr., Day, people remember the African-American civil rights leader.

FEBRUARY

Valentine's Day
On February 14 people send cards and give flowers to people they love.

Presidents' Day
People remember George Washington and Abraham Lincoln.

APRIL

MARCH

St. Patrick's Day
On March 17 Irish-Americans remember St. Patrick. People wear green because it is the color of Ireland.

MAY

Cinco de Mayo
Mexican-Americans celebrate this day on May 5.

Memorial Day
Americans remember people who die in U.S. wars.

JUNE

JULY

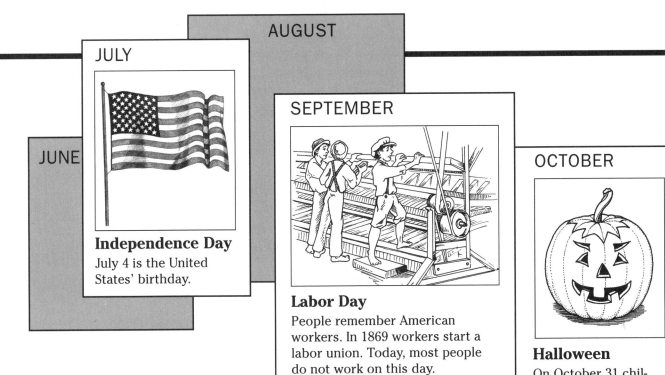

Independence Day
July 4 is the United States' birthday.

AUGUST

SEPTEMBER

Labor Day
People remember American workers. In 1869 workers start a labor union. Today, most people do not work on this day.

OCTOBER

Halloween
On October 31 children wear costumes. They get candy.

NOVEMBER

Veterans Day
On November 11 people remember American soldiers.

Thanksgiving
Families get together and have a big dinner. They eat turkey and pumpkin pie.

DECEMBER

Christmas
On December 25 Christians celebrate Christmas.

Hanukkah
In December Jewish people celebrate Hanukkah.

Quiz

Fill in the blanks with information from *Holidays and Special Days.*

1. New Year's Day is on _____ .

2. Mexicans celebrate _____ _____ _____ on May 5.

3. Families get together and have a big dinner on _____ .

4. The United States' birthday is on _____ . It is _____ Day.

5. The _____ _____ _____ is in January or February.

6. _____ is Valentine's Day.

7. Children wear costumes on _____ .

8. Veterans Day is on _____ .

9. Irish-Americans celebrate _____ _____ _____ on March 17.

10. People remember the African-American leader _____ _____ _____ , Jr., in January.

11. Jewish people celebrate _____ in December.

12. People give gifts on _____ .

13. People remember George Washington and Abraham Lincoln on _____ _____ .

14. Americans remember people who die in U.S. wars on _____ _____ .

NEW YEAR'S DAY

Unit 10

What are the people in the picture doing?

What time is it in the picture?

How do you celebrate the New Year?

Five, four, three, two, one! Happy New Year! It is twelve o'clock midnight. The year ends. A new one begins. Some people are happy. Some people are sad. Everyone thinks about the past year. They hope they are happy in the next year.

New Year's Eve is December 31. It is the night before New Year's Day. People try to be with friends and family. They do not want to be alone. They want to be happy. Many people go to parties or restaurants. Everyone waits for midnight. They eat, drink, and dance. At midnight, people ring bells and blow horns. People say, "Happy New Year!" They kiss and hug.

The biggest New Year's Eve celebration is in New York City. A million people go to Times Square. They wait for the new year. Famous singers sing to the crowd. A large ball slowly comes down from a tall building. Everyone watches it. The new year begins when the ball reaches the bottom. There is a lot of noise. People watch this on television. Many people stay awake until two or three in the morning.

January 1 is New Year's Day. It is a national holiday. People do not work. They stay at home. Most Americans watch television on New Year's Day. In the morning, they watch the Tournament of Roses Parade. Everything in the parade has flowers. After the parade, they watch college football games.

On New Year's Day, many Americans decide to change their bad habits. Some promise to spend less money. Some promise to eat less food. But most people forget about their promises.

VOCABULARY

Match the words and the pictures. Write your answer on the line.

crowd	ring bells	parade
blow horn	hug	celebration

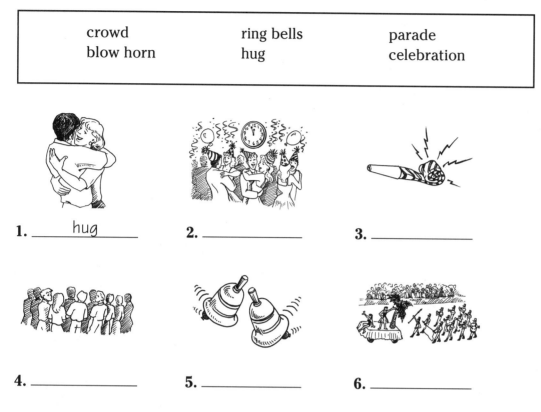

1. _____hug_____

2. _____

3. _____

4. _____

5. _____

6. _____

COMPREHENSION

Understanding the Main Idea

Circle the letter of the best answer.

1. People want to be with friends and family on New Year's Eve because
   a. there are many things to see and do on New Year's Eve.
   b. they do not want to stay home and watch TV.
   c. they do not want to be alone. They want to be happy.

2. At parties, there is a lot of noise at midnight because
   a. there are singers.
   b. people ring bells and blow horns.
   c. people make promises to do good things.

3. On New Year's Day, people watch television because
   a. they like to see parades and football games.
   b. they do not want to be sad.
   c. they want to change their bad habits.

Looking for Details

Circle T if the sentence is true. Circle F if it is false.

		True	False
1.	Americans like to visit new places to celebrate the new year.	T	(F)
2.	People like to go to bed early on New Year's Eve.	T	F
3.	Some people are unhappy if they are alone on New Year's Eve.	T	F
4.	At midnight, people say "Happy New Year!"	T	F
5.	The biggest New Year's Eve celebration is in California.	T	F
6.	Most people work on New Year's Day.	T	F
7.	Many people promise to change their bad habits on New Year's Day.	T	F

ACTIVITY

Interview a partner. Ask these questions:

1. What are two good things from last year?

2. What are two bad things from last year?

3. What do you want to do next year?

Discuss answers with your classmates. Does anyone have answers like yours?

WRITING

Write three promises on the lines.

1. Next year I want to _____

2. Next year I want to _____

3. Next year I want to _____

What is your idea of a perfect year? Write two sentences.

EXAMPLE: _____ I spend a lot of time with my family. _____

1. _____

2. _____

ST. PATRICK'S DAY

Unit 11

What is your favorite holiday?

Does your holiday have a special color?

What do people do on your favorite holiday?

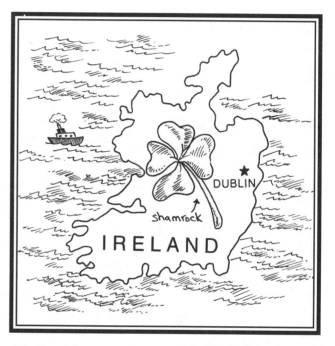

Many Irish people live in the United States. St. Patrick's Day is their holiday. St. Patrick's Day has a special color—green.

St. Patrick's Day is not a national holiday in the United States. But it is a special day. Many people in the United States celebrate it. They remember the Irish people in the United States and Ireland.

Ireland has a lot of green grass. So green is the color of Ireland. Ireland also has a lot of shamrocks. They are small plants with three leaves. If you find one with four leaves, you are lucky. Many people wear shamrocks on St. Patrick's Day.

On St. Patrick's Day, there are parades. People wear green clothes. They sing, dance, and eat Irish food. Some people make green drinks. In Chicago, they color the river green! Big cities with a lot of Irish people, such as New York, Boston, and Philadelphia, have huge St. Patrick's Day parades. The people in the parades wear Irish clothes. Bands play songs about Ireland.

Many years ago, St. Patrick is a priest in Ireland. He teaches the Irish about Christianity. People tell many stories about St. Patrick. One story says there are no snakes in Ireland because St. Patrick sends them away. St. Patrick dies in A.D. 461.

In 1845 many people from Ireland come to live in the United States. They come because Ireland does not have enough food. On St. Patrick's Day the Irish people in the United States remember their country.

VOCABULARY

Draw a line to connect the words that go together.

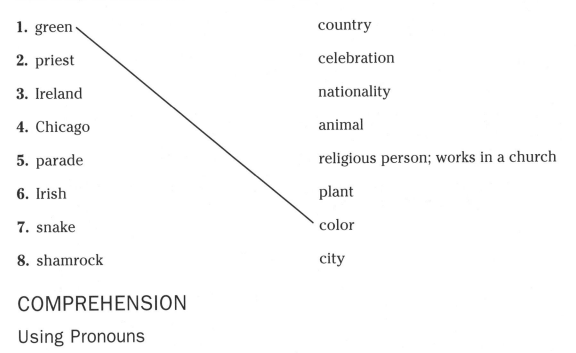

1. green   country

2. priest   celebration

3. Ireland   nationality

4. Chicago   animal

5. parade   religious person; works in a church

6. Irish   plant

7. snake   color

8. shamrock   city

COMPREHENSION

Using Pronouns

Write the letter of the answer that matches the underlined pronoun.

1. But <u>it</u> is a special day. _____*a*_____   **a.**   St. Patrick's Day

2. <u>They</u> are small plants with three leaves. _____   **b.**   snakes

3. <u>They</u> sing, dance, and eat Irish food. _____   **c.**   St. Patrick

4. <u>He</u> teaches the Irish about Christianity. _____   **d.**   shamrocks

5. St. Patrick sends <u>them</u> away. _____   **e.**   people

Looking for Details

Find the best answer to complete the sentence. Write the letter of your answer on the line.

1. Green is the color of Ireland because Ireland _____*e*_____.

2. A shamrock with four leaves is lucky because _____.

3. On St. Patrick's Day, people _____.

4. St. Patrick is important to the Irish because _____.

5. Many years ago, Irish people come to the United States because _____.

a. most of these plants have three leaves

b. wear green clothes and eat Irish food

c. he teaches them about Christianity

d. Ireland does not have enough food

e. has a lot of green grass

ACTIVITY

Interview a classmate about his or her favorite holiday. Talk about a holiday in the United States or another country. Find the answers to these questions:

1. What is the name of your favorite holiday?

2. When do people celebrate the holiday?

3. What do people wear?

4. What do people do?

5. Why is the holiday special?

Tell the class about your partner's special holiday. Write the names of everyone's holiday on the board. Compare them. Which holiday is the most fun? Which holiday is the most interesting?

WRITING

Write five sentences about a special holiday. Write about a holiday in the United States or another country.

EXAMPLE: Thanksgiving is a special holiday. Families get together and eat a
              large meal.

1. _____

2. _____

3. _____

4. _____

5. _____

LABOR DAY

What are the children in the picture doing?
What year do you think it is?
Do you know of any holidays for workers?

The story of Labor Day starts in the 1800s. Men and women work 12 to 16 hours a day. They work 7 days a week. They make very little money. Workers have no benefits. They do not get any money when they are sick. They do not get vacations. Children work, too. Women and children work for very little money in the factories. One of these children is Peter McGuire. He is born in 1852. At age 11 he works in a factory.

The workers want a better life. But they are afraid to ask for better pay. They do not want to lose their jobs. But when workers come together, they are not afraid. When they all ask for benefits, it is easier. Finally, workers come together in labor unions.

The first labor union starts in 1869. The unions help workers improve their lives. Peter McGuire is president of a labor union. He wants a holiday for workers. His dream comes true. The holiday is September 5, 1882. There is a big parade in New York City for all the workers in the United States.

In 1894 Labor Day is a national holiday. Labor Day is always the first Monday in September. Most people do not go to work on this day. They have a three-day weekend. Some people go to the beach. Others have a barbecue or a picnic, or watch the Labor Day parades.

VOCABULARY

Write the correct word in the blanks.

lose	barbecue	factories
benefits	improve	labor unions

1. Workers in the 1800s want to make their lives better. They want to ___improve___ their lives.

2. In the 1800s, women and children work in _____. They make clothes, shoes, and many other things there.

3. Workers are afraid to ask for more money because they will _____ their jobs and not have any work.

4. In 1869 workers finally come together in groups. These groups are called

    _____ .

5. Today's workers get money when they are sick. They get vacations. These are

    examples of _____ .

6. On Labor Day, many people have a _____ outdoors. They cook chicken, hamburgers, or hotdogs over a fire.

COMPREHENSION

Following the Sequence

Which happens first? Write 1 on the line. Which happens next? Write 2 on the line.

1. __1__ Men and women work 14 hours a day. They work 7 days a week.

    __2__ Peter McGuire works in a factory. He is 11 years old.

2. _____ Workers decide to work together.

    _____ Workers want to improve their lives.

3. _____ The first labor union starts in 1869.

    _____ Peter McGuire is president of a labor union.

4. _____ There is a big parade in New York City for all the workers.

    _____ Peter McGuire wants to have a holiday for workers.

5. _____ People go to the beach, have barbecues, and watch parades.

    _____ Labor Day is a national holiday.

Looking for Details

Which sentence is correct? Circle *a* or *b*.

1. **a.** In the 1800s, workers have no vacations.
   b. In the 1800s, workers get money when they are sick.

2. **a.** In the 1800s, women and children work for very little money.
   b. In the 1800s, women and children make a lot of money.

3. **a.** The first labor union starts in 1852.
   b. The first labor union starts in 1869.

4. **a.** Peter McGuire becomes president of a labor union.
   b. Peter McGuire becomes mayor of New York City.

5. **a.** Labor Day is always the first Monday in September.
   b. Labor Day is always on September 5.

ACTIVITY

Work with a partner. Think about the perfect job. Discuss the following questions with your classmates:

1. What is the job?

2. Where is the job?

3. How many days do you work each week?

4. How many vacation days do you have?

5. How much do you earn?

Do many students have the same ideas?

WRITING

Write about the job that you have. If you do not have a job, write about a job you want to have.

EXAMPLE: I am a clerk in a shoe store. I work five nights every week. I start work at 5:30 and leave at 10:00. I like my job because it is close to home. I can walk to work. I also like to meet people.

Part 5

WASHINGTON, D.C.

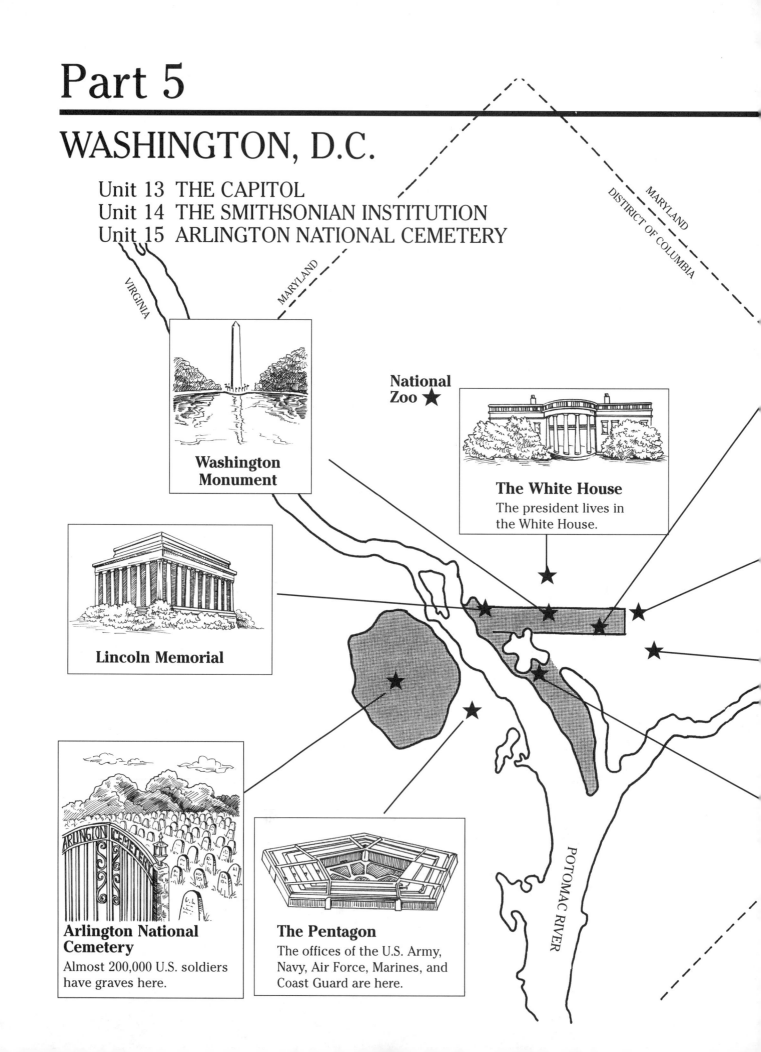

VIRGINIA

MARYLAND

MARYLAND

DISTRICT OF COLUMBIA

Washington Monument

National Zoo ★

The White House
The president lives in the White House.

Lincoln Memorial

POTOMAC RIVER

Arlington National Cemetery
Almost 200,000 U.S. soldiers have graves here.

The Pentagon
The offices of the U.S. Army, Navy, Air Force, Marines, and Coast Guard are here.

The Smithsonian Institution

This is the largest museum in the world.

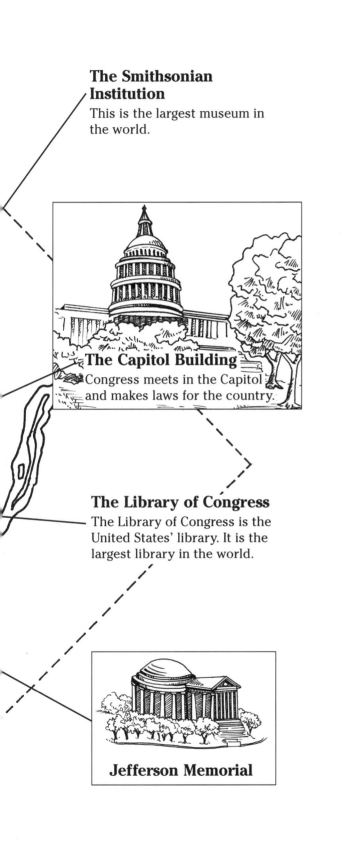

The Capitol Building

Congress meets in the Capitol and makes laws for the country.

The Library of Congress

The Library of Congress is the United States' library. It is the largest library in the world.

Jefferson Memorial

The Stars and Stripes

The red, white, and blue of the United States flag is sometimes called "The Stars and Stripes."

Facts About Washington, D.C.

Washington, D.C., is the capital city. It is not a state. It is a district. The district is called the District of Columbia (D.C.).

1791	George Washington chooses the place for the capital city.
1814	The British burn the White House, the Capitol, and other buildings.
1815	The Americans rebuild the White House, the Capitol, and other buildings.
1912	Japan gives the United States 3,000 cherry trees.
1963	Over 200,000 people come to Washington, D.C. Martin Luther King, Jr., gives a famous speech: "I Have a Dream."
Today	607,000 people live in Washington, D.C.

Quiz

Fill in the blanks with the information from _Washington, D.C._

1. Washington, D.C, is the _____ of the United States.

2. The president lives in the _____ _____ .

3. Almost 200,000 U.S. soldiers have graves in _____ _____

   _____ .

4. The offices of the U.S. Army, Navy, Air Force, Marines, and Coast Guard are in the

   _____ .

5. The _____ _____ is the largest museum in the world.

6. Congress meets in the _____ Building.

7. Members of Congress make _____ for the country.

8. The _____ _____ _____ is the world's largest library.

9. In 1791 _____ _____ chooses the place for the capital city.

10. In 1814 the _____ burn the White House, the Capitol, and other buildings.

11. In 1963 _____ _____ _____ , Jr., gives a famous speech
    at the Lincoln Memorial.

12. In 1912 _____ gives the United States 3,000 cherry trees.

13. The American flag is sometimes called _____ _____

    _____ _____ .

THE CAPITOL

Think of another country. Who tells people what they can and cannot do?

Where do these people work?

What do you know about government in the United States?

The United States Congress works in the Capitol building in Washington, D.C. In the Capitol, members of Congress pass laws for the country. Congress has two parts. One is the Senate. The other is the House of Representatives. Each state elects people to be in Congress. Visitors can watch members of Congress work on laws.

There is a statue on top of the Capitol. It is the goddess of Freedom. When Congress meets, the statue has a light.

Today, the Capitol has 540 rooms. It has restaurants, kitchens, post offices, a barbershop, and a prayer room. Visitors can see many of these rooms. They can also see hundreds of paintings and works of art in the Capitol.

The House of Representatives and the Senate have offices in another building. Underground trains go from their office building to the Capitol. Senators and congressmen have people who work for them. Sometimes these staff members stay in the Capitol building. They call the congressmen and women when something important happens. The congressmen and women come quickly on the train. They get there in time to vote. But this train is not just for members of Congress. You can take this train too.

VOCABULARY

Write the correct word in the blanks.

pass	laws	statue
elect	members	staff

1. Congress decides what citizens can and cannot do. Congress makes _____*laws*_____ .

2. Each state votes to choose the men and women in the Senate and House of Representatives. They _____ them to the Senate and House of Representatives.

3. In order to _____ a law, most of the members of Congress must vote for it.

4. The _____ on top of the Capitol building is the goddess of Freedom. It is a woman made of stone.

5. People who work for a senator are part of the senator's _____ .

6. The congressmen and women are part of Congress. They are _____ of Congress.

COMPREHENSION

Matching

Find the best answer to complete the sentence. Write the letter of your answer on the line.

1. The Capitol building is in ____*c*____ .

2. The members of Congress have very important work. They _____ .

3. The people of each state elect _____ .

4. Visitors to the Capitol can _____ .

5. Staff members sometimes stay in the Capitol. They call the congressmen and women if _____ .

a. members of Congress

b. something important happens

c. Washington, D.C.

d. make laws for the country

e. watch members of the House of Representatives and Senate work on laws

Looking for Details

Circle T if the sentence is true. Circle F if it is false.

		True	False
1.	The Capitol is divided into two parts. They are the Senate and the House of Representatives.	T	(F)
2.	When Congress meets, there is a flag on top of the Capitol building.	T	F
3.	The Capitol has post offices and restaurants.	T	F
4.	Visitors can see some of the rooms in the Capitol.	T	F
5.	Visitors cannot watch the members of Congress work on laws.	T	F
6.	There are many paintings in the Capitol.	T	F
7.	Only members of Congress can take the underground train to the Capitol.	T	F

ACTIVITY

Work in groups. Read these old laws. What do you think about these laws? Should these laws come back? Why or why not?

1. Everybody must take a bath at least once a year.

2. You cannot travel on a bus if you eat garlic.

3. Teachers can hit students.

4. Students pray (talk to God) in the classroom.

5. All businesses are closed on Sunday.

Report your ideas to the class. Which laws should we still have? Which laws should we not have?

WRITING

You are a member of Congress. Write three new laws. Share your laws with your classmates.

EXAMPLE: _People cannot smoke in restaurants._

1. _____

2. _____

3. _____

THE SMITHSONIAN INSTITUTION

Why are museums important?

What museums do you know?

What do you like to see in a museum?

People do unusual things with their money. Some people die and give all their money to their pets. Other people give their money to people they do not know. One rich man, James Smithson, gives everything to a country he does not know—the United States.

The story begins about 150 years ago. James Smithson is a rich British scientist. He never goes to the United States. He has no friends there. But he dies and gives all his money to the United States. No one knows why he selects this country. But they know one thing—Smithson wants his money to start a place where people can learn. The Smithsonian Institution has its first building in 1846. Little by little, the Smithsonian grows. The Smithsonian is in Washington, D.C.

Today, the Smithsonian Institution is the largest museum in the world. The Smithsonian has 13 museums and galleries. It also has the National Zoo. You can learn many interesting things at the Smithsonian. You can learn about American history, art, and technology. At the National History Museum, you can see the first Star Spangled Banner flag. This is another name for the flag of the United States. At the National Air and Space Museum, you can see the first airplane built by the Wright Brothers in 1903. The Smithsonian is the world's most popular museum. About 8 million people go there every year.

Today, the Smithsonian has about 140 million objects. It can take you 265 years to see everything!

VOCABULARY

Write the correct word in the blanks.

objects	galleries	popular
selects	flag	scientist

1. America's _____flag_____ is red, white, and blue.

2. There are many _____ in the Smithsonian. In fact, there are 140 million things to see.

3. Smithson studies plants, animals, and other things. He is a _____.

4. Smithson is British, but he gives his money to the United States. No one knows why he _____ the United States.

5. Many people like the Smithsonian. It is very _____.

6. The Smithsonian Institution has many works of art. You can see them in special buildings called _____.

COMPREHENSION

Following the Sequence

Which happens first? Write 1 on the line. Which happens next? Write 2 on the line.

1. _2_ People give their money to their pets.

   _1_ People die.

2. ____ James Smithson is a rich scientist.

   ____ James Smithson gives his money to the United States.

3. ____ The Smithsonian is the most popular museum.

   ____ The Smithsonian has its first building in 1846.

4. ____ The first airplane flies.

   ____ The first airplane is in the National Air and Space Museum.

5. ____ You can learn many interesting things at the Smithsonian.

   ____ James Smithson wants a place where people can learn.

Looking for Details

Find the best answer to complete the sentence. Write the letter of your answer on the line.

1. The Smithsonian Institution is the largest

   _____.

2. The Smithsonian Institution is in _____.

3. Smithson wants a place where people can

   _____.

4. The Smithsonian Institution has _____.

5. At the National History Museum you can see the

   _____.

6. At the National Air and Space Museum you can see

   the _____.

7. It can take over 200 years to see everything because

   _____.

a. learn about things

b. first United States flag

c. there are about 140 million objects in the Smithsonian

d. museum in the world

e. 13 buildings

f. first airplane

g. Washington, D.C.

ACTIVITY

Work with a partner. Look at the pictures and the words that go with them. You work at a museum. You take people to see the museum. How can you solve each problem?

1. You go to the hotel to pick up the people. One man is not there.

2. The bus breaks down on the way.

3. At the museum two people talk during the lecture.

4. A baby cries. He does not stop crying.

Discuss answers with your classmates. Are any of your answers the same?

WRITING

Imagine you are very rich. You do not have a family. Who or what do you give your money to? Explain.

I want to give my money to _____

because _____

ARLINGTON NATIONAL CEMETERY

Do you like to visit famous places? Why or why not?

Do most cemeteries look like the one in the picture? If no, what is different?

Think of another country. Where are famous people buried?

People usually do not want to visit cemeteries. Most of us never want to go to a cemetery! But some cemeteries have thousands of visitors every year. These cemeteries have important people's graves. There are special monuments and statues and interesting things to read. Arlington National Cemetery is interesting and very beautiful.

Arlington National Cemetery is near Washington, D.C. It is in a beautiful part of Virginia. There are many trees and lots of green grass. Almost 2,000 American soldiers have graves there. The graves of presidents and other important people are also in the cemetery. You can see the grave of President John F. Kennedy. It has a flame that burns all the time. The grave of his brother, Senator Robert F. Kennedy, is nearby. You can also see a tomb for the astronauts who died in the space shuttle *Challenger*.

The famous Tomb of the Unknown Soldier is in Arlington National Cemetery. It has the bodies of three United States soldiers. No one knows who they are. This tomb is for all the U.S. soldiers who die in wars. There is a guard in front of the tomb. He walks up and down in front of the tomb 42 times each hour. Every hour during the day, a new guard comes. At night, a new guard comes every two hours. Thousands of people come to see the "changing of the guard."

VOCABULARY

Match the words and the pictures. Write your answer on the line.

| tomb | flame | monument |
| space shuttle | guard | astronaut |

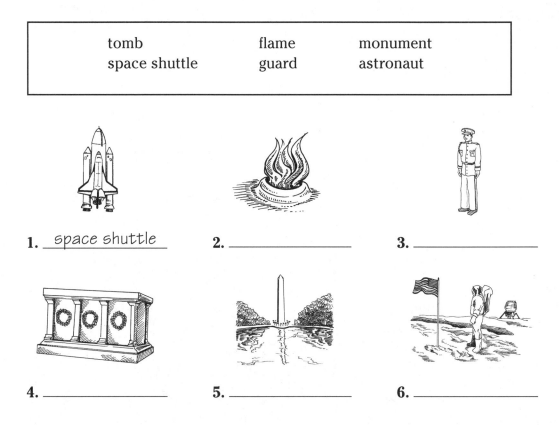

1. _space shuttle_

2. _____

3. _____

4. _____

5. _____

6. _____

COMPREHENSION

Understanding the Main Idea

Circle the letter of the best answer.

1. Many people visit Arlington National Cemetery because
   a. they like to see the trees.
   b. they want to meet special people in the United States.
   c. they want to see an important and interesting place.

2. The Tomb of the Unknown Soldier is important because
   a. people can watch the changing of the guard there.
   b. it is for all the soldiers who die for America.
   c. it has the body of a very famous American.

Looking for Details

One word in each sentence is **not** correct. Find the word and cross it out. Write the correct word or words.

Washington, D.C.

1. Arlington National Cemetery is near ~~Virginia.~~

2. There are many buildings and lots of green grass in Arlington National Cemetery.

3. Arlington National Cemetery has the graves of almost 5,000 American soldiers.

4. There is a statue on the grave of President John F. Kennedy.

5. The cemetery has a tomb for the soldiers who died in the space shuttle *Challenger*.

6. A president walks up and down in front of the Tomb of the Unknown Soldier.

7. At night, a new guard comes every hour to the Tomb of the Unknown Soldier.

ACTIVITY

Write the name of the place you want to visit. Write the name of the place you do not want to visit.

White House	Pentagon	Statue of Liberty
Mount Rushmore	Liberty Bell	Yellowstone National Park

1. I want to go to _____

2. I do not want to go to _____

Share your answers with the rest of the class. Which place is the most popular? Which is the most unpopular? Why?

WRITING

Write about a monument or important place in another country. What is it called? Where is it? What is it for? Why is it important?

EXAMPLE: ___The Parthenon is an important place. It is in Athens, Greece.___

_____

_____

_____

_____

_____

Part 6

U.S. ARTS AND ENTERTAINMENT

ARTISTS

Frank Lloyd Wright

Frank Lloyd Wright is an architect. He makes beautiful, unusual buildings.

Capital, 1939

Isamu Noguchi

Isamu Noguchi is a sculptor. His sculptures are very modern.

Oriental Poppies, 1928

Georgia O'Keeffe

Georgia O'Keeffe paints flowers and modern landscapes.

Grandma Moses

Grandma Moses starts to paint at age 76. Her paintings are simple. Grandma Moses is famous at age 80.

WRITERS

Emily Dickinson

Emily Dickinson is a poet. She almost never leaves her house.

Langston Hughes

Langston Hughes writes poems. A famous poet likes his poems. Langston is famous.

Maya Angelou

Maya Angelou is a modern writer. She writes about her childhood.

Mark Twain

Mark Twain writes about life on the river.

PEOPLE IN ENTERTAINMENT

Ella Fitzgerald

Ella Fitzgerald sings at a contest when she is 15. She becomes a star and travels around the world. People call her the "First Lady of Song."

Steven Spielberg

Steven Spielberg is a movie director. He makes the famous movie *ET*.

Louis Armstrong

Louis Armstrong is a jazz trumpet player. He is the first jazz musician to be famous around the world.

Katharine Hepburn

Katharine Hepburn is a movie star. She is famous for her movies and her clothes.

Quiz

Fill in the blanks with the information from *U.S. Arts and Entertainment*.

1. Frank Lloyd Wright is an _____ .

2. Emily Dickinson is a _____ .

3. Maya _____ writes about her childhood.

4. Isamu Noguchi is a _____ .

5. Steven Spielberg is a _____ _____ .

6. _____ _____ writes about life on the river.

7. Georgia O'Keeffe paints _____ and landscapes.

8. Grandma Moses starts to paint at age _____ .

9. _____ _____ is a jazz trumpet player.

10. People call _____ _____ the "First Lady of Song."

11. Katharine Hepburn is a _____ _____ .

12. Langston Hughes writes _____ .

LANGSTON HUGHES
Unit 16

What do you want to do in your life?

Do your parents want you to do something different?

Do you want to be famous? Why or why not?

Do you hear people say that something good comes from something bad? Sometimes a bad thing happens, but in the end, it is good. This happens to the famous poet, Langston Hughes.

Langston lives in Kansas. His family is very poor. His mother takes him to the nearest school. Most of the children at the school are white. Langston is an African-American. Many of the children do not like Langston because he is black.

Langston is often sad and lonely. He loves poetry, so he writes poems about his feelings. In high school, he writes the best poems in his class. The class chooses Langston as the class poet.

Langston's father wants him to be an engineer. He sends him to Columbia University. But Langston does not like it. He quits school.

Langston does not get a good job. He goes to Washington, D.C., and gets a job in a hotel. He is a busboy. He picks up dirty dishes. Langston is very unhappy. One day, a famous poet comes to the hotel. Langston meets him and gives him some of his poems. The famous poet likes his poems very much. He tells everyone about Langston's poems. The next day, Langston's picture is in the newspaper. People call him "The Negro Busboy Poet." Langston is famous.

Langston moves to New York City. He writes and writes. He writes poems, stories, and plays. He writes for newspapers, too. He writes about African-Americans in the United States. He is one of the first famous black writers. He is very important because he shows people that African-Americans can do great things. He dies in 1967. People today love his writing, too.

VOCABULARY

Write the opposites. You can find the words in the story.

1. happy   <u>S</u>   <u>A</u>   <u>D</u>

2. unknown   ___ ___ <u>M</u> ___ ___ ___

3. last   ___ ___ <u>R</u> ___ ___

4. dies   ___ ___ ___ <u>E</u> ___

5. starts   ___ <u>U</u> ___ ___ ___

6. worst   ___ ___ ___ <u>T</u>

7. takes   ___ ___ <u>V</u> ___ ___

COMPREHENSION

Using Pronouns

Write the letter of the answer that matches the underlined pronoun.

1. <u>They</u> are poor. _____*d*_____

2. <u>He</u> sends him to Columbia University. _____

3. He sends <u>him</u> to Columbia University. _____

4. Langston does not like <u>it</u>. _____

5. Langston meets <u>him</u>. _____

   a. Columbia University

   b. Langston's father

   c. a famous poet

   d. Langston and his family

   e. Langston

Looking for Details

Find the best answer to complete the sentence. Write the letter of your answer on the line.

1. Many of the children do not like Langston because _____.

2. Langston writes poems because _____.

3. The class chooses Langston as the class poet because _____.

4. Langston leaves Columbia University because _____.

5. Langston Hughes is very important because _____.

   a. he writes the best poems

   b. he does not want to be an engineer

   c. he shows everyone that African-Americans can do great things

   d. he is black

   e. he wants to write about his feelings

ACTIVITY

Langston is often sad and lonely. What can people do when they are sad or lonely? Call a friend? See a movie?

Work with a partner. Pretend one of you is sad or lonely. Talk about why you feel this way. The other person gives advice. Tell what your partner can do to feel better. Compare your ideas with your classmates. Who gives the best advice?

WRITING

What do you do? Write your answers on the lines.

1. When I am lonely I

_____

_____

2. When I am sad I

_____

_____

3. When I am happy I like to

_____

_____

GRANDMA MOSES

Think of a famous person. How old is this person?

Why is he or she famous?

Do you think it is better to be famous when you are old or when you are young? Why?

Most people rest and relax when they are old. They do not work. And most people certainly are not famous. But Grandma Moses is different. She starts a new job at age 76 and is rich and famous when she is 85!

As a child, Grandma Moses is Anna Mary Robertson. She is a poor farmer's daughter. She is one of ten children. She works on other people's farms to make money. In 1887 she marries Thomas Moses. He is a farm worker too. They both work on a farm. He dies in 1927.

By now, Anna Mary Moses is over 70 and a grandmother. She embroiders pictures to give to her children. But then she gets arthritis. She cannot embroider anymore, so she paints pictures. She makes paintings of country life. One day, her daughter takes her paintings to a store in town. Her paintings are put in the window. A man from New York sees the paintings in the window and buys them. And he wants more!

The man likes Grandma Moses's paintings. He wants to help her. So he takes her paintings to galleries in New York. Otto Kallir has a famous gallery there. He likes the paintings by Grandma Moses. In 1940 Grandma Moses's paintings are in Kallir's gallery. She is 80 years old.

Grandma Moses suddenly is famous. Everyone wants her paintings. So she paints more and more. She wins many prizes for her paintings. She is famous in the United States and Europe. She is on television, and they make a movie about her.

When she is 100 years old, the state of New York says her birthday is "Grandma Moses Day." Everyone loves this sweet old lady. After her 100th birthday, she makes 26 more paintings. She dies at age 101. She leaves 11 grandchildren, 31 great-grandchildren, and a lot of people who think she is amazing!

VOCABULARY

Write the correct word in the blanks.

amazing	gallery	embroiders
paintings	arthritis	farm

1. Anna Mary works on a _____ . There are many animals and plants. They make milk and food.

2. It is hard for Grandma Moses to move her fingers because she has _____ .

3. Grandma Moses uses thread and a needle. She _____ pictures on cloth for her children.

4. Grandma Moses is an artist. She makes beautiful _____ of life in the country. She uses many colors.

5. A _____ is a place where people sell art. It is like a museum. You can buy the art.

6. Everyone likes Grandma Moses. They think she is very good. They think she is

_____ .

COMPREHENSION

Following the Sequence

Which happens first? Write 1 on the line. Which happens next? Write 2 on the line.

1. _2_ Anna Mary Robertson gets married in 1887.

   _1_ Anna Mary Robertson goes to work on a farm.

2. ____ Anna Mary Moses gets arthritis.

   ____ Anna Mary Moses embroiders pictures to give to her children.

3. ____ Anna Mary Moses paints pictures for her children.

   ____ Anna Mary Moses has her paintings in a store window.

4. ____ Otto Kallir decides to put Grandma Moses's paintings in his gallery.

   ____ A visitor from New York buys Grandma Moses's paintings.

5. ____ Grandma Moses becomes famous in the United States and Europe.

   ____ The state of New York has a special day called "Grandma Moses Day."

Looking for Details

Which sentence is correct? Circle *a* or *b*.

1. **a.** Anna Mary Robertson has ten children.
   (b.) Anna Mary Robertson has nine brothers and sisters.

2. **a.** The husband of Grandma Moses is an artist.
   b. The husband of Grandma Moses is a farm worker.

3. **a.** Anna Mary paints pictures when she is 12.
   b. Anna Mary paints pictures after she is 70.

4. **a.** Anna Mary's daughter takes her mother's paintings to a store.
   b. Anna Mary asks the store owner to put her painting in the window.

5. **a.** Otto Kallir sees the paintings in the store window.
   b. A man who buys the paintings shows them to Otto Kallir.

6. **a.** Grandma Moses becomes world famous.
   b. Grandma Moses is famous only in the United States.

7. **a.** Grandma Moses paints when she is over 100 years old.
   b. Grandma Moses paints her last painting on her 100th birthday.

ACTIVITY

Work with a partner. Ask your partner what he or she wants to do after age 65.

start a new job	work on hobbies	play sports
travel	live somewhere special	be famous

Share answers with your classmates. Do many students have the same answers?

WRITING

Who is the oldest person you know? Write five sentences about this person. What do you like about the person? What does he or she do?

EXAMPLE: _My great-grandfather is the oldest person I know. He is kind and sweet._

1. _____

2. _____

3. _____

4. _____

5. _____

ELLA FITZGERALD

Do you like to sing? If so, what kind of music do you sing?

Can one day change a person's life? Why or why not?

Do you want to change your life? How?

Sometimes a person's life changes very quickly. Suddenly, everything is different. Ella Fitzgerald has this kind of life.

When Ella is a young child, her parents die. She grows up in an orphanage in New York. At age 15, she enters a contest in New York. For the contest, she wants to sing and dance. But Ella gets very nervous and she cannot dance. So she just sings.

Ella does not know the contest is going to change her life. A famous jazz musician named Chick Webb is in the audience. He is looking for a new singer for his band. When he hears Ella's voice, he gives her the job.

Chick Webb and his wife take care of Ella. They teach her to be a good singer. Ella travels with his band. In 1938 Ella writes a song with Chick Webb. This song is a great success. Ella is a star.

Chick Webb dies, but Ella sings with his band for three more years. Then she sings alone. She travels all over the world. She has an amazing voice. She can sing any kind of song. People who like rock music like her. So do people who like jazz.

Ella sings for almost 60 years. She sings over 2,000 different songs. She sells over 25 million records and sings with more than 40 orchestras. People call her the "First Lady of Song." Ella dies in 1996. But people always remember Ella's voice.

VOCABULARY

Write the correct word in the blanks.

musician	contest	orphanage	nervous
star	orchestra	audience	

1. Chick Webb plays music and sings songs. He is a ___musician___ .

2. Ella is very famous. Everyone knows about her. She is a _____ .

3. Ella lives with other children who do not have parents. They all live in an _____ .

4. Ella and many other girls try to be the best singer. They are in a _____ .

5. Before Ella sings, she is scared. She is _____ .

6. Many people watch Ella sing. They are the _____ .

7. A large group of people play music and Ella sings with them. They are the _____ .

COMPREHENSION

Understanding the Main Idea

Circle the letter of the best answer.

1. One contest changes Ella's life because
   a. an important person hears her sing.
   b. she finds a man and woman to take care of her.
   c. people see her dance.

2. People call Ella the "First Lady of Song" because
   a. she sings with the great musician Chick Webb.
   b. she is a famous singer for almost 60 years.
   c. she writes a song and it is a big success.

Looking for Details

Circle T if the sentence is true. Circle F if it is false.

	True	False
1. Ella grows up in a famous theater in New York.	T	(F)
2. Ella knows she will be famous after she wins a contest.	T	F
3. Chick Webb is famous before Ella is famous.	T	F

4. Webb wants a new songwriter for his band.   T   F

5. Ella becomes a star after she writes a song with Chick Webb.   T   F

6. Ella is famous only for her jazz singing.   T   F

ACTIVITY

Discuss the following questions with a classmate:

1. What is your favorite kind of music?

2. Who is your favorite male singer?

3. Who is your favorite female singer?

4. Who is your favorite group or band?

5. What is your favorite musical instrument?

Share answers with your classmates. What kind of music is the most popular? Which performers are most popular?

WRITING

Look at the pictures below. Make sentences with the words under the pictures. Write one or two sentences for each picture. Write your sentences on the lines.

1. Ella/grow up/ orphanage/New York

2. Famous musician/ Chick Webb/want/ Ella/sing/band

3. 1938/Ella/write/ song/with Webb

4. Webb/die/Ella/ sing/all over world

1. _Ella grows up in an orphanage in New York._ _____

2. _____

3. _____

4. _____

Part 7

THE STORY OF AMERICA

In 1783 the British lose the war. The United States is born. George Washington is the first president.

In the 1600s many British people come and live in North America. The British king makes their laws. The Americans want to be free. The War of Independence begins in 1775.

In 1492 Christopher Columbus comes from Spain. He stops on an island near America.

From 1865 to 1900 many people come to the United States from Europe.

In 1861 there is war between the North and the South. It is the Civil War. The war ends in 1865. The North wins.

Slaves work on farms in the South. They are not free. John Brown helps the slaves.

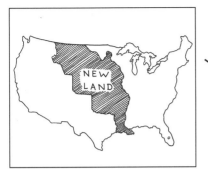

In 1803 President Thomas Jefferson buys land from France.

In 1869 people build the first railroad across the country.

The army makes Native Americans live in special places called *reservations*. Sitting Bull is a Native American leader. He fights the army.

In the 20th century, the United States fights World War I, World War II, the Korean War, and the Vietnam War.

In the 1960s African-Americans want civil rights. They want equality. Their leader is Martin Luther King, Jr.

In 1969 Neil Armstrong is the first person on the moon.

In 2000 . . .

Quiz

Fill in the blanks with information from *The Story of America*.

1. In 1492 _____ _____ lands on an island near America.

2. The people in America want to be free from _____.

3. The War of Independence begins in _____.

4. The United States is _____ in 1783.

5. _____ _____ is the first president.

6. In 1803 _____ _____ buys land from France.

7. In 1869 people build a railroad _____ the country.

8. The army makes the Native Americans live on _____.

9. _____ _____ is a Native American leader.

10. In the South, _____ work on the farms.

11. The Civil War between the North and the South begins in _____.

12. The _____ wins the Civil War.

13. _____ _____ _____, Jr., is the leader of the African-Americans who want their civil rights.

14. Neil Armstrong walks on the moon in _____.

PAUL REVERE'S RIDE

Who is a famous hero in the United States or another country?

Why is he or she famous?

Do you want to do what this person does? Why or why not?

It is 1775. People live in colonies. They are not free. The king in England makes their laws. They pay taxes to the king. They do not want to pay money. And they want to be free. The men in the colonies get ready to fight the British. People call them "Minutemen" because they can be ready to fight in a minute. They hide guns in the town of Concord, Massachusetts.

The British soldiers are in Boston. They know the Americans have guns at Concord. So they decide to go to Concord.

Paul Revere is an American colonist. He knows that the British are going to Concord. But Revere does not know which road they are going to use. It is important for him to know the correct road. He must tell the Minutemen. Then they can stop the British.

A friend helps Revere. The friend goes to the top of a church in Boston. Revere tells him to send a signal. If the British go on one road, show one light. If they go on the other road, show two lights. Revere waits. Then he sees two lights. He knows which road the British are on.

Revere jumps on his horse. He rides very fast. He tells the people in the villages, "The British are coming! The British are coming!" The Minutemen come to Lexington. They fight the British. The Americans win. This is the first fight of the American Revolution.

VOCABULARY

Write the correct word in the blanks.

jumps	hide	colonies	British
colonists	rides	signal	

1. Revere's friend shows two lights. This _____signal_____ tells Revere something.

2. The people from England are the _____.

3. The people in America are not free. They live in _____.

4. Paul Revere is standing on the ground. He sees the two lights. Then he _____ up on his horse.

5. In 1775 _____ such as Paul Revere and the Minutemen live in the colonies. The king makes their laws.

6. The Minutemen _____ their guns. They do not want the British to find the guns.

7. Paul Revere _____ his horse from Boston to Lexington.

COMPREHENSION

Using Pronouns

Write the letter of the answer that matches the underlined pronoun.

1. <u>They</u> know the Americans have guns.

2. <u>He</u> knows that the British are going to Concord.

3. <u>They</u> fight the British.

4. Revere tells <u>him</u> to send a signal.

   a. The Minutemen

   b. The British soldiers

   c. Revere's friend

   d. Paul Revere

Looking for Details

Complete each sentence with the correct word or words. Write the letter of your answer on the line.

1. The Minutemen hide guns in ___*d*___ .

2. Paul Revere is an American _____ .

3. Revere's friend sends a signal from _____ .

4. Revere's friend sends a signal. He shows _____ .

5. Revere rides through the villages and tells people that _____ .

6. The first fight of the American Revolution is in _____ .

a. two lights

b. the top of a church

c. the British are coming

d. Concord

e. Lexington

f. colonist

ACTIVITY

Why do people today pay taxes? Which taxes are good? Which are bad? Talk with a partner. Do you have the same or different ideas?

WRITING

Write about five important events in your life.

EXAMPLE: _My first day in school is an important event in my life._

1. _____
2. _____
3. _____
4. _____
5. _____

JOHN BROWN

Describe the man in the picture.

Can a person be a hero and a bad person too?

Can you think of a famous person who is a hero to some people and a bad person to others?

In the 1800s slaves work on the large farms in the South. People in the North want the slaves to be free. Some people in the North help the slaves escape.

John Brown lives in the North. He is a good man. He works hard for his family. He also helps slaves escape.

John Brown wants to help the slaves. He decides to fight to free the slaves. In 1859 Brown is 60 years old. He goes to Harper's Ferry, Virginia. His sons and 15 other men go with him. They go to a government building. There are guns in the building. Brown and his men go into the building. They kill some people. The next day, John Brown is still there. He can escape, but he does not go anywhere. He waits for the slaves to help him. He wants them to fight for freedom.

But nobody comes. Then, U.S. soldiers come. Ten people die. John Brown is hurt. The soldiers take him away. Brown has a trial for murder. The court decides that he is a killer. They kill John Brown.

John Brown wants to do something good. But he does bad things. Can a person be both good and bad? Some people think he is a bad person. Other people think he is a hero. Everybody remembers him.

VOCABULARY

Write the correct word in the blanks.

trial	hurt	escape
murder	slaves	

1. Some slaves in the South want to leave the South. People in the North help them

   _____escape_____ .

2. John Brown does not die at Harper's Ferry, but he is _____ .

3. At John Brown's _____ , people in the court talk about what he does. They decide that he is a killer.

4. The people in the South own other people. They own _____ .

5. John Brown kills some people. It is _____ .

COMPREHENSION

Matching

Find the best answer to complete the sentence. Write the letter of your answer on the line.

1. People in the North want __d__ .

2. John Brown helps ____ .

3. The court decides that ____ .

4. John Brown does not escape from the building in

   Harper's Ferry because ____ .

a. John Brown is a killer

b. slaves escape

c. he waits for the slaves

d. the slaves to be free

Looking for Details

Which sentence is correct? Circle *a* or *b*.

1. **a.** In the 1800s people in the South have slaves. *(circled)*
   b. In the 1800s people in the North have slaves.

2. **a.** John Brown wants to fight to free the slaves.
   b. John Brown wants to talk to people about slaves.

3. **a.** When he goes to the building at Harper's Ferry, Brown is alone.
   b. When he goes to the building at Harper's Ferry, Brown has his sons and 15 other men with him.

4. **a.** John Brown is hurt in a fight with U.S. soldiers.
   b. John Brown dies in a fight with U.S. soldiers.

ACTIVITY

Work with a partner. One of you is John Brown. Tell why you want to go to Harper's Ferry. The other is John Brown's friend. Do you want him to go? Tell why or why not.

WRITING

John Brown does good things and bad things. Write two good things he does and two bad things.

EXAMPLE: _John Brown works hard for his family._

1. _____

2. _____

3. _____

4. _____

SITTING BULL

Describe the man in the picture.

What do you know about Native Americans?

In the 1800s many people want land to live on. They go west. They are called *settlers*. More and more settlers move west. But the Native Americans live there, too. The settlers and Native Americans fight. Both Native Americans and settlers die. The U.S. government wants peace in the country. They decide to put the Native Americans on reservations. Reservations are special places where the Native Americans must live. Many do not want to live on reservations. They are very angry. Sitting Bull is the leader of a tribe of Native Americans. He is angry, too.

General Custer is a famous general in the U.S. Army. He has 600 soldiers. He wants to make the Native Americans live on a reservation. In 1876 his soldiers fight Sitting Bull's men. General Custer and all his men die. This fight is the famous Battle of Little Big Horn.

The Native Americans win an important fight. But it is not enough. There are many more soldiers. The Native Americans go north to Canada. But it is cold in Canada. They miss their home. Sitting Bull decides to go back. He gives himself up to the U.S. Army. He is a prisoner for two years.

In 1885 Sitting Bull is a famous person. People say he is a great leader. He wants his people to be happy. Finally, the government decides to free Sitting Bull. Years pass. Sitting Bull is still the strongest Native American leader in the country. The government is afraid Sitting Bull can hurt the settlers. So they arrest him. Men go to his house. There are shots. Sitting Bull is dead. The year is 1890. The name Sitting Bull lives forever in American history.

VOCABULARY

Write the correct word or words in the blanks.

tribes	still	arrest	peace
gives himself up	shots	settlers	prisoner

1. The _____settlers_____ come from many different places. They want to build homes and farms on Native American land.

2. The government does not want to fight. They want _____ .

3. Sitting Bull tells the U.S. Army he does not want to fight any more. He goes to them and
_____ _____ _____ .

4. There are many groups of Native Americans. Sitting Bull is the leader of one group. The groups are called _____ .

5. The government has Sitting Bull in prison. He cannot go away. He is a _____ .

6. Men want to take Sitting Bull to prison. They go to _____ Sitting Bull at his house.

7. Even after many years, Sitting Bull does not change. He is _____ a great leader.

8. Someone fires a gun. The _____ kill Sitting Bull.

COMPREHENSION

Understanding the Main Idea

Circle the letter of the best answer.

1. The Native Americans and the settlers fight because
   a. there is not enough food for everyone.
   b. the Native Americans do not want to live on reservations.
   c. the settlers want to live on the Native American land.

2. Sitting Bull and his men fight the U.S. Army because
   a. the army wants to put them on a reservation.
   b. the army wants to build things on their land.
   c. the army does not want Sitting Bull to be a great leader.

Looking for Details

One word in each sentence is **not** correct. Find the word and cross it out. Write the correct word or words.

1. More and more settlers move ~~east~~ *west* and take Native American land.

2. Reservations are special places where the settlers must live.

3. Custer is a famous president in the U.S. Army.

4. In 1885 Custer and all his men die in the famous Battle of Little Big Horn.

5. Sitting Bull's tribe goes north to Minnesota.

6. Sitting Bull gives himself up to the U.S. reservations.

7. Sitting Bull is a prisoner for three years.

ACTIVITY

Work with a partner. One student is a Native American leader. The other student works for the U.S. government. Both of you want peace. How do you solve the problem? Share your ideas with your classmates. Can anyone solve the problem?

WRITING

How is your life today different from Native American life in the 1800s? Next to each fact about Native American life, write about your life today.

Native Americans hunt for food.   I get food at _____

Native Americans cook over fires.   _____

Native Americans walk everywhere.   _____

Native Americans make their own clothes.   _____

Do you want to live like the Native Americans in the 1800s? Why or why not?

EXAMPLE: *I do not want to live like the Native Americans in the 1800s. They hunt for food. I do not like hunting.*

1. _____

2. _____

3. _____

ANSWER KEY

PART 1 THE UNITED STATES

Quiz **1.** 50 **2.** 250 **3.** Washington, D.C. **4.** Alaska
5. Mississippi **6.** Washington
7. Minnesota **8.** Arizona
9. Alaska **10.** Pacific
11. Delaware **12.** California
13. South Dakota
14. Minnesota **15.** Florida
16. Hawaii **17.** Florida
18. Iowa **19.** corn, beef, milk
20. Texas **21.** Alaska **22.** Idaho
23. oil **24.** Wisconsin
25. Hawaii

Unit 1

Vocabulary **1.** swamp
2. theme park **3.** astronauts
4. alligators **5.** palm trees
Understanding the Main Idea **1.** a **2.** b
Looking for Details **1.** g **2.** d
3. c **4.** a **5.** f **6.** b **7.** e

Unit 2

Vocabulary **1.** smoke
2. erupted **3.** salmon **4.** cut down **5.** volcanoes **6.** forest
Past and Present **1.** name—named **2.** call—called
3. erupt—erupted **4.** turn—turned **5.** die—died
Looking for Details **1.** F **2.** F
3. F **4.** T **5.** F **6.** T

Unit 3

Vocabulary **1.** carnival
2. woodcutter **3.** skyways
4. flows **5.** sculptures
Using Pronouns **1.** d **2.** a
3. c **4.** e **5.** b
Looking for Details **1.** b **2.** b
3. b **4.** a **5.** a

PART 2 U.S. INVENTIONS AND INVENTORS

Quiz **1.** telegraph **2.** Jonas Salk **3.** 1903 **4.** television
5. Thomas Edison **6.** dishwasher **7.** helicopter **8.** telephone **9.** Benjamin Franklin

10. 1892 **11.** traffic light
12. 1937 **13.** Kodak **14.** Robert Jarvik **15.** sewing machine

Unit 4

Vocabulary **1.** a lot **2.** learns
3. none **4.** start **5.** buy
6. ready-made **7.** wealthy
8. retires
Understanding the Main Idea **1.** b **2.** c
Looking for Details
1. ~~immigrant~~/actor **2.** ~~eight~~/eleven **3.** ~~three~~/two **4.** ~~buy~~/sell
5. ~~France~~/England

Unit 5

Vocabulary **1.** amazing
2. saucers **3.** company
4. servants **5.** lovely **6.** break
Following the Sequence
1. 2, 1 **2.** 2, 1 **3.** 2, 1 **4.** 2, 1
5. 1, 2
Looking for Details **1.** a **2.** a
3. a **4.** b

Unit 6

Vocabulary **1.** crowded
2. produce **3.** timer **4.** imaginative **5.** helmet **6.** nightmare
Following the Sequence
1. 2, 1 **2.** 1, 2 **3.** 2, 1 **4.** 2, 1
5. 1, 2
Looking for Details **1.** ~~1975~~/
1875 **2.** ~~rich~~/poor **3.** ~~helmet~~/
belt *or* ~~1901~~/1914 **4.** ~~buys~~/sells
5. ~~watch~~/medal **6.**
~~helmets~~/traffic light

PART 3 U.S. ORIGINALS

Quiz **1.** Strauss **2.** Federal Express **3.** Reader's Digest
4. Coca-Cola **5.** Wrigley
6. Corn Flakes **7.** peanut butter
8. Tuxedo Park **9.** Gillette
10. Avon **11.** potato chips
12. Superman **13.** Xerox
14. crossword puzzle
15. McDonald's

Unit 7

Vocabulary **1.** dream
2. borrow **3.** disappointed

4. milk shakes **5.** enough
Following the Sequence
1. 1, 2 **2.** 2, 1 **3.** 2, 1 **4.** 2, 1
5. 1, 2 **6.** 1, 2
Looking for Details **1.** ~~West~~/
East **2.** ~~salads~~/french fries
3. ~~Boston~~/Chicago
4. ~~service~~/food **5.** ~~five~~/two
6. ~~unhappy~~/happy

Unit 8

Vocabulary **1.** artist **2.** planet
3. lucky **4.** situation **5.** hero
6. ordinary **7.** comic books
Matching **1.** e **2.** a **3.** d **4.** b
5. c
Looking for Details **1.** T **2.** F
3. T **4.** F **5.** F **6.** T **7.** T

Unit 9

Vocabulary **1.** eating tool—
fork **2.** job—chef **3.** snack
food—potato chips **4.** state—
New York **5.** vegetable—potato
6. feeling—mad **7.** direction—
north **8.** list of food—menu
9. machine—automatic peeler
Understanding the Main Idea **1.** b **2.** c
Looking for Details **1.** a **2.** b
3. b **4.** a **5.** b

PART 4 HOLIDAYS AND SPECIAL DAYS

Quiz **1.** January 1 **2.** Cinco de Mayo **3.** Thanksgiving **4.** July 4/Independence **5.** Chinese New Year **6.** February 14 **7.**
Halloween **8.** November 11 **9.**
St. Patrick's Day **10.** Martin Luther King **11.** Hanukkah **12.**
Christmas **13.** Presidents' Day
14. Memorial Day

Unit 10

Vocabulary **1.** hug **2.** celebration **3.** blow horns **4.** crowd
5. ring bells **6.** parade
Understanding the Main Idea **1.** c **2.** b **3.** a
Looking for Details **1.** F **2.** F
3. T **4.** T **5.** F **6.** F **7.** T

Unit 11

Vocabulary **1.** green—color **2.** priest—religious person; works in a church **3.** Ireland—country **4.** Chicago—city **5.** parade—celebration **6.** Irish—nationality **7.** snake—animal **8.** shamrock—plant

Using Pronouns **1.** a **2.** d **3.** e **4.** c **5.** b

Looking for Details **1.** e **2.** a **3.** b **4.** c **5.** d

Unit 12

Vocabulary **1.** improve **2.** factories **3.** lose **4.** labor unions **5.** benefits **6.** barbecue

Following the Sequence **1.** 1, 2 **2.** 2, 1 **3.** 1, 2 **4.** 2, 1 **5.** 2, 1

Looking for Details **1.** a **2.** a **3.** b **4.** a **5.** a

PART 5 WASHINGTON, D.C.

Quiz **1.** capital **2.** White House **3.** Arlington National Cemetery **4.** Pentagon **5.** Smithsonian Institution **6.** Capitol **7.** laws **8.** Library of Congress **9.** George Washington **10.** British **11.** Martin Luther King **12.** Japan **13.** "The Stars and Stripes"

Unit 13

Vocabulary **1.** laws **2.** elect **3.** pass **4.** statue **5.** staff **6.** members

Matching **1.** c **2.** d **3.** a **4.** e **5.** b

Looking for Details **1.** F **2.** F **3.** T **4.** T **5.** F **6.** T **7.** F

Unit 14

Vocabulary **1.** flag **2.** objects **3.** scientist **4.** selects **5.** popular **6.** galleries

Following the Sequence **1.** 2, 1 **2.** 1, 2 **3.** 2, 1 **4.** 1, 2 **5.** 2, 1

Looking for Details **1.** d **2.** g **3.** a **4.** e **5.** b **6.** f **7.** c

Unit 15

Vocabulary **1.** space shuttle **2.** flame **3.** guard **4.** tomb **5.** monument **6.** astronaut

Understanding the Main Idea **1.** c **2.** b

Looking for Details
1. ~~Virginia~~/Washington, D.C. **2.** ~~buildings~~/trees **3.** ~~5,000~~/2,000 **4.** ~~statue~~/flame **5.** ~~soldiers~~/astronauts **6.** ~~president~~/guard **7.** ~~hour~~/two hours

PART 6 U.S. ARTS AND ENTERTAINMENT

Quiz **1.** architect **2.** poet **3.** Angelou **4.** sculptor **5.** movie director **6.** Mark Twain **7.** flowers **8.** 76 **9.** Louis Armstrong **10.** Ella Fitzgerald **11.** movie star **12.** poems

Unit 16

Vocabulary **1.** sad **2.** famous **3.** first **4.** lives **5.** quits **6.** best **7.** gives

Using Pronouns **1.** d **2.** b **3.** e **4.** a **5.** c

Looking for Details **1.** d **2.** e **3.** a **4.** b **5.** c

Unit 17

Vocabulary **1.** farm **2.** arthritis **3.** embroiders **4.** paintings **5.** gallery **6.** amazing

Following the Sequence **1.** 2, 1 **2.** 2, 1 **3.** 1, 2 **4.** 2, 1 **5.** 1, 2

Looking for Details **1.** b **2.** b **3.** b **4.** a **5.** b **6.** a **7.** a

Unit 18

Vocabulary **1.** musician **2.** star **3.** orphanage **4.** contest **5.** nervous **6.** audience **7.** orchestra

Understanding the Main Idea **1.** a **2.** b

Looking for Details **1.** F **2.** F **3.** T **4.** F **5.** T **6.** F

PART 7 THE STORY OF AMERICA

Quiz **1.** Christopher Columbus **2.** Britain **3.** 1775 **4.** born **5.** George Washington **6.** Thomas Jefferson **7.** across **8.** reservations **9.** Sitting Bull **10.** slaves **11.** 1861 **12.** North **13.** Martin Luther King **14.** 1969

Unit 19

Vocabulary **1.** signal **2.** British **3.** colonies **4.** jumps **5.** colonists **6.** hide **7.** rides

Using Pronouns **1.** b **2.** d **3.** a **4.** c

Looking for Details **1.** d **2.** f **3.** b **4.** a **5.** c **6.** e

Unit 20

Vocabulary **1.** escape **2.** hurt **3.** trial **4.** slaves **5.** murder

Matching **1.** d **2.** b **3.** a **4.** c

Looking for Details **1.** a **2.** a **3.** b **4.** a

Unit 21

Vocabulary **1.** settlers **2.** peace **3.** gives himself up **4.** tribes **5.** prisoner **6.** arrest **7.** still **8.** shots

Understanding the Main Idea **1.** c **2.** a

Looking for Details **1.** ~~east~~/west **2.** ~~settlers~~/Native Americans **3.** ~~president~~/general **4.** ~~1885~~/1876 **5.** ~~Minnesota~~/Canada **6.** ~~reservations~~/Army **7.** ~~three~~/two